C000049224

CLOSING
ADDRESS

Copyright © 2022 Impact Publishing®

All rights reserved. No part of this book may be used or reproduced in any manner whatsoever without prior written consent of the author, except as provided by the United States of America copyright law.

Published by Impact Publishing®, Lake Mary, FL.

Impact Publishing® is a registered trademark.

Printed in the United States of America.

ISBN: 979-8-9862097-1-5
LCCN: 2022916812

This publication is designed to provide accurate and authoritative information with regard to the subject matter covered. It is sold with the understanding that the publisher is not engaged in rendering legal, accounting, or other professional advice. If legal advice or other expert assistance is required, the services of a competent professional should be sought. The opinions expressed by the authors in this book are not endorsed by Impact Publishing® and are the sole responsibility of the author rendering the opinion.

Most Impact Publishing® titles are available at special quantity discounts for bulk purchases for sales promotions, premiums, fundraising, and educational use. Special versions or book excerpts can also be created to fit specific needs.

For more information, please write:
Impact Publishing®
P.O. Box 950370
Lake Mary, FL 32795
Tel: 1.877.261.4930

CLOSING ADDRESS

By
Vernon Behrens De Lima, S.C.

Impact Publishing®
Lake Mary, Florida

CONTENTS

PREFACE

To illustrate the visibility of my career in the Trinidad and Tobago Law Courts, most particularly in criminal defense, I think the following comment is revealing:

One day, about twenty years ago, I walked into my Bank to cash a cheque when a little boy standing with his mother, pointed at me and said, "Mummy, look Dole Chadee Lawyer!"

ACKNOWLEDGEMENTS

I would like to thank the following folks who stuck with me all the time, encouraging and motivating me to write this book:

Winston Dookeran, Robert Mayers, Freddie Penco, Merlin Samlalsingh, Joe Hadeed, Wendy Wharton, Karen De Lima, Kathy Govia, Jackie Alston, Alan Agostini and my two sons Damon and Kyle Behrens De Lima. I am blessed to have you as my friends and family.

I love you and thank you all.

CHAPTER 1

ALLOW ME TO INTRODUCE MYSELF

I was born on the 4th of August 1940 in Trinidad.

My parents are Alfonso Behrens De Lima and Audrey Behrens De Lima. My dad was a jeweler, he was the grandson of the famous Yldefonso De Lima, a Sephardic Jew who arrived in Trinidad from Spain in 1884, and established the Firm known as Y. De Lima which is still in existence. I am told my mother was beautiful as a young woman and I believe that. She certainly was a very beautiful mother to me. She was born in Trinidad, the fourth of five children of John and Isabelle Knox, and when she was six years old, the family migrated to the United States of America – New York, where she grew up. She was a very bright person and had she not married my father, I have no doubt that she would have excelled in whatever discipline she chose. But she chose to be Daddy's partner, and that she remained for twenty-four years until his death in 1967.

I attended Mother Lydia's Kindergarten School in St. Joseph Convent in Port of Spain from 1946 to 1949, after which I went to St. Mary's College and then on to Mount St. Benedict – where I completed my secondary education – before going off to London, England to study medicine in 1957.

17

I am the second in a family of five children. Alfonso Behrens De Lima Junior is my older brother. He was born exactly one year before me. Then there are my two sisters, Zilah and Sandra, who arrived shortly after me, and then Ricky, who came after the girls. Ricky was an airline pilot who lost his life tragically in a crash in Guadaloupe in 1991. He was a lovely person and to this day I have difficulty coping with his tragic demise. But, that is life.

My Dad wanted me to be a doctor. This was because of his close friendship with Sir Henry Pierre (known as Joe Pierre), his childhood friend, who was an eminent surgeon in Trinidad. Because of that friendship and because of my love for Daddy, I agreed to become a doctor and I was actually assured of a place to study at St. Bartholomew's Hospital in London as soon as I passed the first MB examination, but that was not to be.

In fact, when I was studying at a Crammers School in London, the principal, Mr. Coleman, a dear old gentleman, asked me whether I really wanted to be a doctor. He obviously had spotted me, and I told him the truth that I really wanted to study law. Thereafter, I wrote to my Dad informing him of my decision. Three weeks later, I received a telegram from him: "SON, BETTER BE A GOOD LAWYER THAN A BAD DOCTOR. LOVE DAD."

On July the 9th 1957, I sailed for England aboard the S.S. Southern Cross, a tourist ship that carried about five hundred passengers, which left Australia bound for England. About fifty Trinidadians, including myself, were picked up when she docked in Port of Spain as her last stop before Southampton. It took ten days for the ship to reach England, and those ten days were probably among the most important ten days of my life; because it was then I was introduced to adult sex, homosexuality, greed and dishonesty – life in the most startling ways. There and then I saw real life for the first time.

18

The voyage lasted ten days and by the time we docked I was about five years older. I had my first girlfriend, a beauty from New Zealand named Judy. She was about three years older than me, but she never knew that. In fact, I always looked about three years older than I really was because I was then already six foot three. Judy was a budding ballet dancer on a scholarship to the Royal Academy of Dance in Battersea, London. We remained good friends for years though she dropped me like a hot potato when she discovered that I was only sixteen. She said people would say she was robbing the cradle. I was sad but glad. And so, I moved on.

London was a great place to be in the late fifties. Of course, all of us from the West Indies in those days experienced discrimination, sometimes in very subtle ways. For at that time, whenever we tried renting a room in London the landlord or landlady very often would ask on the telephone where we were from, and if they found out we were West Indian, that would be that; the room was already taken... end of story. Sometimes the rental notices would read: 'No Dogs, No Blacks, No Irish.' As a result of this and other forms of discrimination, there was a close bonding between the Caribbean people in England; e.g., Jamaicans would stand up for, and sometimes even fight for, other West Indians, against the Teddy Boys. In those days, the Jamaicans were respected because they were not prepared to take bullying from anyone and they made that pellucidly clear. And good for them and for all the rest of us. And the Irish loved us, and we loved them too.

With the help of my guardian, Derek Marcano, who was a Trinidadian studying aeronautical engineering in England, I found and rented 'digs' (a student's room) at No. 7 De Vere Gardens in Kensington, London. My rent was then five pounds a week. Today it would be impossible for a student to rent a room anywhere near De Vere Gardens because that is now considered prime residential area. Anyway, my landlady, when I moved in, was a kind and gentle Irish lady named Mrs. Anna

Carraway, whom I called "Mrs. C". She lived in the basement of the building, which was five stories high, and over the years until I Ieft England in 1965, she was like a mother to me. She was already in her sixties when I met her. She lived there with her daughter, Maris, and her granddaughter, Anna. Mrs. C., like all good Irish folks enjoyed a touch of beer and wine, and so did I, so very often we would sit and enjoy each other's company over a pint of bitter. She was a lovely person and liked nothing better than to give you the gossip of the day in her own inimitable style. Very often I would accuse her of having 'kissed the Blarney Stone'. I miss her very much. We remained friends for many years after I left England. I do know that she returned to Ireland where she died in the late seventies. I also know that she would have been so proud of me for pursuing my profession for fifty years.

Many a time, when I was despondent with my studies, when everything seemed to be going wrong, Mrs. C. would cheer me up and urge me on, reminding me not to give up, but instead to fight on regardless. The word 'surrender' was unknown to her, and she taught me the meaning of resolution. In the breaks from law school, I did many jobs. I sold Bibles door to door and I sold washing machines – the brand was called 'Vactric'. I was introduced to these endeavors by my friend Michael Rodriguez, who was quite a character and a good man.

In the five or six years I remained at No 7 De Vere Gardens, I had at least three girlfriends. Mrs. C. knew them all, but she very diplomatically never mentioned a preference for any of them. However, when I introduced her to Jennifer in 1968, she immediately announced to me, "That is the girl for you, Vernon! The rest of them can't hold a candle to her!" She just loved Jennifer from the moment she met her. So did I.

I have to say that Jennifer Maureen Behrens De Lima, nee Boos, is to me the most important person I ever met in my life. It is to her that I attribute any distinction that I may have attained. When I qualified as a lawyer, I resolved that I would never marry. My father though, knew Jennifer as a child, and he would always say to me that she was the type of person I should marry.

When I first met her in London she detested me, because she said I was conceited and felt I was the cat's whiskers. That was in 1963. I never saw her again until I returned to Trinidad qualified in 1965. I was staying for a week with my parents at Gittens Bay in Monos, down the Islands, when a boatload of my friends came across from Gasparee to visit, and among them was my darling Jennifer. Needless to say, she sat very quietly the whole time assessing the situation. I was very diplomatic this time and by the time her party left at about 6:00 pm to return to Gasparee, I had made up my mind that she would be my wife.

Two weeks later, I telephoned her and asked for a date. She bluntly refused. I felt really badly, but I waited another two weeks and called again. This time she agreed, and we began dating. That was fifty-two years ago. We got married on the 25th of June 1968 and we remained together until the 24th of January 2016, when she died.

Our marriage took place in a lovely Catholic Church on Church Street, Kensington High Street, London, England. There were just nine guests at our wedding, but to us it was a beautiful wedding. At the time, I was *persona non grata* with her mother, as a result of which there were no members of her family present at the ceremony. What is more, her three brothers tried their best to dissuade us from marrying, telling us that the marriage would be doomed because we did not have the blessing of Jennifer's parents. This all came about because her mother, who was strong willed, wanted to take control of our lives very early on. However, both of us being equally strong minded, were adamant that we would not allow it. I must say though, that my mother-in-law, Marjorie Pierre, turned out to be a wonderful person to me and my family. We loved and respected her and she us, and the relationship could not have been better.

Jen and I on Our Wedding Day

Jennifer was a tower of strength, fortitude and bravery all her life. No one, not even I, ever dared to tell her what she had to do. And I am very proud to say that those qualities have been passed on to each of our four children. She stood up at all times for what was right and renounced what was wrong, and she was never afraid to announce openly her stand on any matter whatsoever. We enjoyed so many pursuits together, including horse racing, fishing, crab catching, crayfish catching, and disguising our children at Carnival to name but a few.

Throughout our marriage, Jennifer and I called each other "Honey" and some of our friends made a joke of this. Like all marriages we had our up-and-down times, but we were happy and loved each other like mad. Those forty-eight years were the happiest years of my life—thanks to Jennifer.

I really could not have asked for a better mother-in-law. She was kind to us and she was a great influence on our children. Added to which, Sir Henry, whom we affectionately called "Uncle Joe", became my dear, dear friend and remained so until he passed in 1980 in England. I played the quatro and sang the calypso, which I learnt to do when I was a student in England, and Uncle Joe loved it when I sang the old time calypsos like 'Mary Ann', and 'In a Calabash', and 'The Graf Zeppelin' and many more. Very often we would light up a party with our music when things were getting a little dull and it was a great way of bringing everybody together; those who couldn't play the quatro 'could hit bottle or spoon', thereby enhancing the rhythm, bounce and the beat of the music. It was nothing but beautiful, and it was the way we Trinis lived and partied. And even better fun if you added a little rum to the proceedings. Hence the song: 'Rum and Coca Cola'. Indeed, on the night Uncle Joe passed, I played the tune 'Bam Weh Onti Bo' for him on the quatro minutes before he passed.

I passed the UK Bar examination in late 1965, and I returned to Trinidad and was 'called to the Bar' there in November

1965. My father was the proudest man of all. He was a lovely man who had educated himself by worldly travel. He was a jeweler by profession, but more important to him was his love for people who would come from far and wide to speak with him about their problems, as he sat at his desk in his store, The Trinidad Jewelry Limited.

As a child, he was known as "Popito" and later on in life was called "Alfonse". I am told that when he was a bachelor, he was a real ladies man. He was a very good dancer of the tango and Joropo and Spanish Waltz. He dabbled in local politics and counted among his friends many famous political personalities of the day, like Dr. Eric Williams, Albert Gomes (whom we affectionately called "Uncle Bertie"), Sir Alexander Bustamante from Jamaica, Joito Vialva from Venezuela, Sir Grantley Adams of Barbados and Teddy Marryshow from Grenada.

Daddy was a good actor and many a time he would recount stories of old Trinidad and the legal luminaries of the day like Sir Edgar Gaston Johnson, K.C., Mr. Scipio Pollard, K.C. and Mr. Louis Wharton, K.C., and he would actually act out how they dealt with clients and the courts.

A case in point: Sometime in the 1930s, a man was charged for petty larceny in the Chaguanas Magistrates' Court. He retained Mr. Scipio Pollard, K.C. to defend him. On the morning of his case, Mr. Pollard arrived at court about ten minutes before the Court convened. Pollard was a most imposing man, he was about 6 ft. 5 in. tall, with a deep baritone voice, had a handlebar moustache and always wore a three-pieced suit. He really was a most imposing man. But he was also a man of the world. He understood people and I am told he was a most kind and generous man.

Anyway, to get back to the story. Mr. Pollard's client informed him that the witness had not yet arrived, whereupon Mr. Pollard began walking up and down the verandah of the Court where all the people were sitting, and he kept pulling on his moustache and saying to himself, aloud, "Hmm! I don't like the sound of this! Today, today, somebody have to go to jail!"

Needless to say, when the case was called at 9:45 am the witness had still not arrived, and the case was dismissed.

My Dad also had great respect and admiration for Sir Lennox O'Reilly, into whose Chambers I would go. There were three O'Reilly brothers, Sir Lennox, Guy and Harry, and they came originally from St. Lucia where their father was a schoolteacher. All three of them excelled in the law in Trinidad and Tobago. Sir Lennox was a brilliant advocate who was known as 'the man with the silver tongue' for obvious reasons, and he was also a member of the Legislative Council. He was known as 'Lap O'Reilly' by his friends because his full name was Lennox Arthur Patrick O'Reilly.

A most imposing man who stood 6'4" and commanded respect as soon as he entered a room, Guy his brother was a renowned conveyancer and kept himself to that. It is said that he was the force behind Sir Lennox, who was a socializer *par excellence*, and very often never got home until dawn. So it was his brother Guy who did all the devilling and preparation of the briefs, and the man with the silver tongue would merely present the argument to the Judges, all of whom had the highest respect for him.

And then there was Harry. Harry was a magistrate, and then became Registrar of the High Court of Trinidad.

I was always interested in the criminal law. In the 50's, we had the cases of Boysie Singh and Dr. Dalip Singh. I was only twelve or thirteen at the time, but like everybody else, I was engrossed in all that was written and/or said about these cases. Boysie was a notorious man. He was first charged together with four other men with the murder of one Philbert Peyson (alias 'Bumper').

This case went to trial in 1952 and Boysie and his accomplices were convicted. However, six weeks after the trial, the Court of Appeal quashed the conviction and released them all. I recall that Boysie's lawyer was Mr. Rupert Archibald, whom I have always considered to be the best criminal lawyer that I ever knew – and I knew a lot of them. He was wise, gracious and eloquent, but at the same time humble. I consider it a real honor to have met this man. I was so fortunate to be his junior in two matters in San Fernando in the seventies. He was so good, and truly brilliant, and he taught me so much.

A few months after Boysie Singh was acquitted, Dr. Dalip Singh went on trial for the murder of his wife, Dr. Inge Singh, and he was convicted.

In 1956, Boysie Singh was again charged with murder. This time the allegation was that he and one Bolan Ramkissoon willfully murdered Bolan's common law wife, Thelma. This time the Crown was represented by Mr. Malcolm Butt, Q.C. and Mr. Ralph Hercules. Boysie was represented by Sir Edgar Gaston Johnson, K.C. and Bolan by Mr. Issac Hyatalie. The trial Judge was Mr. Justice Fabian J. Camacho, a very good friend of my father, and one of the most independent and fair-minded persons you could ever meet. It was a real travesty that he was never appointed to be Chief Justice, but in those colonial times subterfuge was the order of the day, and even best friends were encouraged to knife one another in the back to get to the top.

I was only a very young man when this trial took place, but I maneuvered my way into the courtroom to hear the closing addresses. And what a lasting impression that would have on my life! Firstly, Mr. Hyatali. He was most eloquent as he put his case fairly to the jury. Then Mr. Butt addressed. And then

Justice Camacho summed up the case. The verdict was guilty. And both Bolan and Boysie were sentenced to hang for this murder. They were indeed hanged for that crime.

A few months after Boysie was convicted, I was invited by Justice Camacho to accompany him to a murder trial in the Port of Spain Assizes. I was fifteen years old at the time, and was home for vacation, so I readily accepted. I was allowed to sit in the court where I could see all that was going on. The man on trial was named Fitzroy Carr, and he was accused of murdering his common law wife. The trial lasted two days and he was found guilty. I vividly remember what occurred thereafter; everyone in the court except the judge was made to stand and then Justice Camacho donned a black cloth over his wig and proceeded to read the death penalty to the prisoner. Thereafter, he broke the nib of his pen by smashing it into the desk. I was absolutely dumb-struck by what I had witnessed, and the impression has remained with me up to today.

THE DEATH PENALTY SENTENCE

Prisoner at the Bar (John Thomas)

You have been found guilty of the Offence of Murder.

The Sentence of this Court is, that you be taken from where you stand

To a place of lawful execution.

And there, at a date and time appointed by the President of the Republic

You suffer death by Hanging.

And May the Lord Have Mercy on Your Soul.

CHAPTER 2

A LAW STUDENT IN LONDON

In the late 1950's, I was a law student in London. I must say that those days were not easy for us West Indians. We faced discrimination and prejudice at every turn, and we got the brunt of the English feelings.

I recall the case of Curtis Pierre, a Trinidad panman[1] who was the captain of the 'Dixieland Steel Band' which had gone to England for a stint. One night, Curtis was walking on his way home when a car stopped, and he was accosted by two plain clothes policemen who insisted on searching him, whereupon they found a small starting pistol in his pocket. They immediately arrested him and took him down to Station and charged him with possession of a firearm. One has to remember that this happened at a time when the racial problems were at the highest in London, with the Teddy Boys reigning and discrimination was at its highest. Nottinghill Gate had just taken place and it was dangerous to be a West Indian in London.

Among the giants who stood up for us Trinidadians in England at the time was Sir Learie Constantine. Sir Learie was firstly

---

1. A musician in a Steel Band orchestra in which instruments are known as 'pans'

a perfect gentleman, secondly, a true West Indian, and thirdly, a really great cricketer. I met him on several occasions, and I say truly that he is among the five greatest people I have ever known. He was, like Mr. Rupert Archibald, a truly humble man. You would never know if you met him that he was a great man, because like Sir Henry Pierre and Mr. Rupert Archibald, he exuded humility. I really don't know what has happened to people nowadays why that quality has disappeared altogether. I feel so sorry for our children that they will never know people like Sir Hugh Wooding, or Mr. Rupert Archibald, or Sir Learie or Sir Henry or Mr. Bruce Procope. I am sorry that they will not know what they were like in life.

Now that they are gone, the students are left to believe that they must have been like our present day leaders—like politicians or lawyers or even our star cricketers. What a misconception!

I can tell you, unequivocally, that none of those four men would subscribe to many things that are considered the norm nowadays. It may be that these days people are more concerned with material wealth than with what they are able to contribute to the society to make it better.

Trinidad is a lovely little island in the West Indies. It is about ten miles east of Venezuela, hence the tremendous impact that that country has on our island. Over the years, Venezuelans would flee to Trinidad whenever there were political problems in that country, and there are so many ways in which our society has been, and continues to be, influenced by Venezuela.

Our music is a fine example of what I mean, with the parang[2] music which we play every Christmas that is sung in pidgin Spanish which is similar to patois which is, of course, pidgin French spoken by most of our older fisher folk.

The population of Trinidad and Tobago is said to be 1.3 million,

---

2. Local or folk music

and that figure, for some mysterious reason, has remained the same for the last fifty years. It is widely believed however that the true figure is nearer two million. The people of Trinidad are by and large very beautiful people, we have produced one Miss World and two Miss Universes, would you believe? We are very intelligent people as well, and we excel wherever we go in the world – whether it is in sport or science, the arts or in music or whatever. It is remarkable that such a small island has produced so many internationally-recognized persons over the past fifty years.

Names like Sir Vidya Naipaul, Dr. Eric Williams, Joseph Lennox Pawan, Sir Learie Constantine, Sir Hugh Wooding, Sonny Ramadhin, Lennox Pierre, Brian Lara, the Mighty Sparrow, Lord Kitchener, Audrey Jeffers, Janelle Penny Commissiong, Giselle Laronde, Wendy Fitzwilliam, Calypso Rose, Jeffrey and Boscoe Holder and so many others all come from Trinidad. They excelled in their disciplines and did our country proud. All hats off to them!

When I returned to Trinidad from England in November 1965, I was fortunate to be accepted into the Chambers of Mr. Guy O'Reilly, Q.C. at 11 St. Vincent Street in Port of Spain. Mr. O'Reilly had by that time retired because of health issues, but he lived in his home at No 5 Maxwell Phillip Street, St. Clair, and he was always available to me. He was a lovely man, and I had the feeling then that he knew all the law by heart. He was so kind and gentle, and insisted that I should call him on the telephone whatever time I wanted to, but I never did.

Vernon was 'called to the Bar' in 1965

CHAPTER 3

I MEET MY LEARNED FRIENDS

I was twenty-five years old and a newly-qualified Barrister-at-Law, just recently admitted to the Bar. I had a seat in the Chambers of Mr. Guy O'Reilly, Q.C. which was then headed by Mr. Bruce Procope, Q.C. It was awesome for me. James Davis, popularly known as Jim, was the most senior of Mr. Procope's juniors, and there was also Miss Sheila Teelucksingh, who had trained for several years under Sir Guy, and was one of the outstanding conveyancers of the country. She never entered a court room in all the years I knew her, but she was respected by the entire profession. The one other junior at the time was Trevor Bertie, who was a lovely person, smoked incessantly and was always giving jokes.

When I entered those chambers in 1965, Mr. Bruce Procope, Q.C. was without dispute one of the outstanding Barristers (now called Attorneys) in Trinidad and Tobago. He was in great demand by all the big companies of the day. I felt at the time that he was getting ready to take over the gauntlet from Sir Hugh Wooding, Q.C. who was undoubtedly the king of them all. Mind you, there were many other outstanding senior civil lawyers at that time as well, such as Mr. Algernon Pope Wharton, Q.C., Mr. Lionel Seemungal, Q.C., Mr. Hamel Wells, Q.C., Mr. Henry

Hudson Phillips, Q.C., and Mr. Tajmool Hosein, Q.C. And to boot, in those days there were so many brilliant young advocates just waiting to take their rightful place in the profession – such as Michael De Labastide, Alan Alexander, Ewart Thorne, Otis Alcala, Sonny Maraj, Russel Martineau, and Frank Misir. I felt humbled and in awe to be a colleague, believe me.

Recently, I asked a friend of mine why did she think there were so many outstanding lawyers in those days and no longer. She did not know and neither do I. But it is a fact. Verily, I cannot think of one lawyer in Trinidad today who could conceivably match wits with Sir Hugh Wooding, or with Clement Phillips, or with Telford Georges, or Aubrey Fraser. The standard of the Bench was so very high that many a young lawyer would be in awe whenever he or she had to appear in the High Court, much less the Court of Appeal. I remember well that in those days, judgments of the Court of Appeal were delivered verbatim the minute an appeal was concluded. One of the three judges would deliver the ruling of the court, and the palantypists sitting below the judges would transcribe the judgment as it was being delivered. That practice disappeared many years ago with the watering down of the judiciary.

Nowadays, a court of appeal judgment takes about six weeks to be delivered if you are lucky. And all the beautiful speeches about how many cases are concluded annually really amount to hog wash. The backlog of criminal cases now is unreal, and as I write there are at least eight hundred persons languishing in Golden Grove Prison awaiting trial for murder. This is unacceptable particularly when one remembers that only about fifty of those persons will have their matters resolved in court every year. Couple this situation with the poor police work these days and one realizes at once the serious situation that exists.

The backup of capital cases will undoubtedly lead to prison chaos very soon, if it hasn't already started, and to crown it all is the blatant disregard that the authorities show for the men and women who have to face trial in the assizes. It is almost as if they couldn't care less, as long as they are not inconvenienced in any way. It is the typical 'I'm all right, Jack' attitude. It is so sad really.

We have laws that are on the books but are never carried out. By statute, murder is punishable by death in Trinidad and Tobago. Section 4 of our Offences Against the Persons Act states that, "Every person convicted of murder shall suffer death." But since Dole Chadee and his associates were executed in June of 1999, and one other person, Anthony Briggs, a few weeks later, the death penalty has not been carried out. It is a farce really, and I actually was sitting in court one day when the judge passed sentence of death on a man who began laughing aloud. The judge asked him why he was laughing, and he responded, "Because you know damn well they don't hang anybody in this country!" That is the kind of disrespect the criminals have for the law and law-abiding citizens.

I have said for years that the only people who carry out the death penalty in Trinidad and Tobago are the criminals, and they have no compunction about doing it, and what is more, they are even allowed to appeal to a Mercy Committee that is available to them, but the law-abiding citizen has no such entitlement. And would you believe that that Committee is still in existence up to this day, irrespective of the fact that no one is ever hanged. So, the criminals are in charge of the system. And they know and understand that very well.

This situation took a while to evolve, and the various Governments, instead of dealing with the problem as soon as it raised its head years ago, aided and abetted it by introducing various pieces of legislation that not only impeded the quick flow of justice, but also assisted the criminal to the extent that his rights superseded those of the ordinary good and law-abiding citizen.

Furthermore, we must remember that we are locked in to the English judicial system which really has become irrelevant to us in Trinidad. But for some unknown reason, we are afraid to 'grab the bull by the horns' and say: "Thank you very much for your help over the years, but we can go it alone now!" And leave them with their liberal legal procedures that they believe is good for England, and allow us to decide what are the laws and procedures we consider to be relevant and proper for Trinidad and Tobago today.

It is a total mess. A criminal trial that would have taken three days to complete ten years ago now takes two months. Imagine what impact this has on the entire system. Work the math. If there are ten criminal courts functioning all the time and each case takes two months, how many cases can we complete in a year.

But I digress. I really want to tell you about my journey as a barrister-at-law in Trinidad and Tobago, and of all the interesting people, good and bad, I met along the way and how they impacted my life. I think it is important that I do this more particularly because most of the criminal lawyers of my time have gone and none of them left any writing whatsoever. Karl Hudson Phillips, Q.C. died three years ago in London. Teddy Guerra, S.C. died in 2016. Desmond Allum, S.C. died in 2015 and Aeneas Wills, S.C. and Frank Solomon, S.C. died last year. All of them were outstanding lawyers, and I am grateful that I was friendly with them. Over the years we worked on the same side sometimes, and at other times we worked against one another. But there was always respect for one another in whatever we did, and we remained friends to the end.

I can say without any question that in those days the expression, 'my learned friend', meant exactly that. And over the years, I accumulated many 'learned friends'. Among them were Jessel Hannays, Jim Davis, Rawlston Nelson, Clive Phelps, Lennox Sanguinette, Shastri Moonan, Aldwyn Prevatt, Trevor Bertie,

Sheila Teelucksingh, Sandy Mason, Nizam Mohammed, Reno Ramgoolam, Clem Razack, Neville Hordatt, Nazimodeen Mohammed, David Patrick, Joseph Pantor, Dana Seetahal, Rajiv Persad, Alice Soo Hon, Faraaz Mohammed, Ravi Rajkumar, John Heath, Patrick Godson Phillips, Joseph Marcano, Henry Debe, Hugo Ghany, Massa Khan, the brothers Charles and John Tyson, Oudit 'Doc' Ramlogan, Chris Nath, Basdeo Toolsie, Herman Bholai, Carlyle Walters, Natty King, Maillard Howell, Selwyn Mohammed, Gillian Lucky and so many others. These were not only good lawyers, but good people. I was privileged to know them all. These were truly 'my learned friends'.

As I said before when I started out, the lawyers of the day were more than willing to help a young lawyer to catch himself. My dear friend Reno Ramgoolam, who I knew in London, was the one who started me out in Trinidad. When he learned that I had returned, he called me right away and made arrangements for me to come to Point Fortin to do a few cases with him. Can you imagine what that meant? I would go down there and appear with Reno for people charged before the magistrate and very often he would leave the cross-examination to me. Mind you, he would be present and looking on and guiding me as I went. And of course, I never left Point Fortin without a few dollars which were my fees. It was an unbelievable start to my career. And of course, Mr. O'Reilly was thrilled with the arrangement, because he would tell me that if I had to make mistakes, it was better to make them in Point Fortin and not in Port of Spain.

I would drive my small car (which was loaned to me by my dear friend, Bobby Johnson) to Point Fortin two days a week for the next eight to ten months, and it was one of the most enjoyable periods of my career. I got to know most of the restaurant owners there, and in the hunting season we would have wild meat for lunch before returning to court for the afternoon session. And very often, the policemen who were appearing in the court as prosecutors would sit and have lunch with us in the restaurant, such was the respect we always had for one another. But as fate would have it, I was forced to give up my Point Fortin practice because things were heating up in Port of Spain and I was needed there.

Country court practice was great and I shall never forget it. This was how it worked: You were obliged to hire a 'clerk' whom you were expected to pay 20% of whatever fee he fixed for your labour. And that was that. When you attended the office (which was twice a week), your clerk would be ready to introduce you to the clients, with the briefs typed out, and of course with your fee in cash for each brief. It was a wonderful practice and I enjoyed it immensely.

I shall never forget receiving my very first fee in Port of Spain. It was $500.00 paid to me by Y. De Lima & Company for an opinion about Pawnbroking, and to me it was like manna from Heaven. I am sure my uncle, Jack De Lima, was responsible for arranging that. He was a good and kind man.

Mr. Guy O'Reilly K.C. (my friend and mentor)

CHAPTER 4

MY FIRST
HIGH COURT CASE

Sometime around the latter part of 1966, I was retained to represent a man from Diego Martin whose name was Cecil Glaud, a young farmer who was charged for rape. I readily accepted the brief and in the month of October the trial began in the Port of Spain 4th Assizes Court, presided over by Mr. Justice Kester McMillan. The prosecutor was Mr. Clinton Bernard.

After only two days, the jury returned a verdict of guilty, and my client was sentenced to five years hard labour. This was a most important experience for me, because I really thought that he would be acquitted, and when the sentence was read to him I felt as though it was being imposed on me. It was a rude awakening for me, and I swear from that day I never ever was cocksure about what a jury would do in a criminal case. I felt so certain in my mind that Glaud would be acquitted that I could hardly speak when I was called upon in the allocutus stage to "say anything as to why sentence should not be passed." I was numb.

For a whole week I was unable to sleep because I thought I had done something wrong, and that that was why we lost. I was miserable, and so I went to visit Mr. O'Reilly at his home. I was ushered into his bedroom where he was lying on the bed. We greeted each other and I immediately told him what had happened. He looked at me for about ten seconds and then he said, "Look here, young man. You are an advocate. You will present your case according to the instructions in your brief. What the court decides to do after you have done your bit is its concern and not yours. I hope I have made myself clear. What is more, if you cannot sleep because of the verdict then my advice to you is give up the criminal law altogether. Because you must be prepared to walk from one court into another, and another if need be, for different clients, with the knowledge that you have done your best for each of them in turn, as you go. Do you understand me?" I said that I did and I meant it. I walked out of his home that afternoon and I never looked back.

About eight weeks after Glaud's trial, the appeal came on and the Court of Appeal allowed it. The Court held that there was no direction by the trial judge about the uncorroborated evidence of the woman, and so the appeal was allowed, the conviction quashed, and Glaud was freed. Today, that case would take at least three weeks to complete, and the appeal would come up about three years later.

Most people, when they meet a criminal lawyer ask the same question, "How can you defend a person who you know is guilty?" It is not an unreasonable question. But then most people do not really understand how the criminal law works. They believe the accused tells his counsel everything including whether he has committed the crime. In fact, that rarely happens because if an accused reveals to his counsel that he has done the crime and yet he wishes to allege he was elsewhere when it was done, the lawyer would be in contempt of court if he should permit that, because he would know that the defence is a lie and he would be considered to be part of that lie. But accused persons are well aware of this and many of the prisoners have over the years become knowledgeable of the criminal law and procedure, so that they give preliminary advice to their fellow prisoners before even their family has retained a lawyer.

So the prisoners discuss the case in the remand yard and many times the defence is actually contrived and moulded and/or constructed right there. Sometimes the seasoned prisoner would say to the novice accused, "So, tell me, who is going to be your lawyer?" Whereupon the accused would say, "I think it's either Guerra or De Lima!" Then the graduate would respond, "Don't make the mistake and tell them lawyers that you really do it you know; because if you do that they go drop the case!" So, the charade then begins. The lawyer is retained and visits the prison where he takes a statement from the accused, and that statement is signed by the accused as his own, and thereupon becomes his instructions to the lawyer.

Thereafter, both lawyer and client are bound by those instructions. It is a vital document for the lawyer because should the accused at a later stage complain to the court that he suffered an injustice because of his lawyer's incompetence in presenting his case, the lawyer would be entitled to reveal the contents of his instructions which were signed by the client as his own. It is therefore very dangerous and irresponsible for an attorney not to take a full and comprehensive signed statement from a client before starting a case, because should that client become under sufficient pressure at any time, (which is very likely to happen in a criminal case), he is inevitably going to blame his lawyer. That's a given.

CHAPTER 5

MY FIRST MURDER APPEAL CASE

Sometime around the end of August 1967, I received a short letter from a man in the condemned cells in the Royal Gaol. His name was Hector Bentick and the letter read:

> *Sir, I am writing you these few lines, Sir, for you to pay me a visit at the Royal Gaol. I am a prisoner condemned to die for a crime which I have not committed, and on these grounds, Sir, I hold you very high in esteem with regards to your profession, hence the reason for I writing you. Sir, I would like you to pay me this visit as early as possible, because time is very short.*

> *I remain,*
> *Your Obedient Servant.*
> *Hector Bentick*

I was really intrigued by his letter, and so I went to visit him in the condemn cells in the Royal Gaol, Port of Spain, the same day. I was eager to go there because I was fast and wanted to see where condemned prisoners were kept and the conditions under which they were held, etc.

Imagine my dismay when the prison officer escorting me

upstairs to see Bentick produced a bunch of very large keys and began searching for the one which would fit the door leading to the cells. After a lot of clanging noises, he opened it and I was able to see and assess the entire scenario. There were about twenty cells on the left and another twenty on the right. Each cell had a very heavy door which seemed to me to be made of purple heart or some other hard wood. About three quarters up the door and in the middle there was an aperture about eight inches square, which was itself covered with mesh wire, through which the prisoner could look and talk. Imagine that. This was 1967 and I really felt that I had been taken back 100 years. I was afraid, but more than that, I was so saddened by what I saw.

I couldn't believe at the time that human beings existed like those condemned men did. But more important was what it said about our judicial system. It seemed to me that the attitude was that once you were found guilty of a crime, then you would have to be incarcerated in the most dehumanizing way because that is what you deserved and that is what we do to such people, regardless of whether you might succeed in your appeal, if you had one. I was stunned. And I immediately thought of *Papillon* and what he had experienced in French Guiana.

Anyway, Bentick, a broom-maker from Gasparillo, was convicted of murdering 15-year old Anne Marie Bachan, also of Gasparillo, on the 21st of November, 1964. He was tried three times for that murder. Convicted in the first trial, he appealed and was granted a retrial. The jury failed to agree in the retrial so another retrial was ordered, and this time he was convicted and sentenced to death.

The first thing I said to him was that I had never done an appeal and so I didn't understand why he would write to me. He said that was all right, and that he was confident I would win his case.

We spoke for about half an hour and it was agreed that I would do the appeal. He admitted that he had no money at all, but he promised to have his sister, who was a market vendor in San Fernando, deliver to me ten pounds of tomatoes which would constitute my fee. I agreed and began studying his case.

It was a case that depended entirely on circumstantial evidence, because no one ever saw Bentick interacting with the girl. The evidence was that he was seen walking up a road about 200 feet behind her, and that was the last time she was seen alive. Her body was found floating in a lagoon nearby a few hours after she was last seen. She had been strangled. As a result, the case was called 'The Case of the Gasparillo Strangler'.

In the notes of evidence of the trial, there appeared an item that went into evidence as an exhibit that was never identified. It was a blood-stained panty. Nowhere in the notes was there any mention of how this came about, who produced it or to whom it belonged. The entire appeal was based on this one fact, and I made that submission. It caused a great furor when it was advanced because the court could not believe that there was no explanation for this item. In fact, they stood down the case and sent for the police complainant who was stationed in San Fernando. Three hours later he testified that he really could not say where the panty had come from. That was that, the appeal was allowed and Bentick was freed.

But there is an interesting aftermath to this case and I give it as I remember it. When I went to the condemned cells after the decision, and I told Bentick that he had succeeded and would be freed that day, he fainted, and the prison officers had to attend to him to resuscitate him. I was asked to stand aside whilst this was done and the other condemned prisoners began chanting the hymn *Amazing Grace*, and then *Glory, Glory, Hallelujah!*

On my way back down the steps from the condemned cells to the courtyard, the guard who accompanied me said this to me,

"Well, well, Sir, I now can say I see everything. Three years ago, when Bentick came into prison on this charge, he told me that he would be freed one day, but that the lawyer who would do his case successfully was still a student abroad, but he would be coming back to Trinidad qualified soon." I tell it as I remember it.

What is more, Bentick never paid my fee. I never received the tomatoes he promised. And about ten years later I was doing a murder case in the San Fernando Assizes, and during the lunch break, a man walked up to me in the verandah and said, "Boss, you remember me?" I really didn't have the slightest idea who he was and then he said, "I am Bentick!" I replied, "Oh yes, Hector. I am told that you have done well, and that you own a fleet of taxis. Good for you, but I must remind you that you never paid my fee. I never got the tomatoes." His reply was, "Boss, the publicity my case gave you was more than any money I could pay you. So, you was well paid, ok?" I bowed and walked away, and I never saw him again. That was a very good lesson for me as a young criminal lawyer. To understand well that once you have finished a criminal case, that is that. Whatever fees may be outstanding are forgiven, for they will never be paid; and more than that, if that client should ever again need a lawyer he will avoid you, because he owes you.

That was a lesson taught to me by no other than the great Mr. Rupert Archibald, Q.C. and his dear wife Ruby, who drove him from Court to Court, for years.

But Bentick was right about one thing. His case did catapult me immediately. The morning after the Court of Appeal gave its decision, I was bombarded by people wanting me to do their cases. The waiting room in our Chambers was filled with waiting clients. It was really remarkable, but I was well and truly on my way.

CHAPTER 6

IN THOSE DAYS AUTHORITY PREVAILED

In those days, Trinidad was a very different place from what it is today. There was a sense of authority that prevailed, and everyone was very conscious that the law was to be respected and obeyed, and that there were serious consequences that would follow if it were to be broken. The penalty for murder was death by hanging, and that punishment was carried out without any serious delay. On an average, it would be fair to say that from incident to execution was usually about twelve months.

As for crimes of violence such as vicious assaults with intent to inflict serious bodily harm as well as rape and the like, if found guilty, the trial judge was empowered to impose a sentence of corporal punishment in addition to whatever term of imprisonment he deemed appropriate. Such sentence was carried out at the Carrera Prison under the supervision of the Prison doctor. The accused persons were most afraid of the 'Cat-o'-Nine Tails' and very rarely would someone who received it return to crime.

And that is a fact. It was administered one-third at the beginning of the term, one-third halfway through the term, and the final one-third just before the end of the term. Even hardened criminals feared that penalty.

On the 11th of October 2017, His Holiness Pope Francis declared that the death penalty is "inappropriate no matter how serious the crime committed." His Holiness continued, "It is inadmissible because it attacks the inviolability and dignity of the person."

I am a practicing Roman Catholic, and I must abide by the teachings of my Church even if I disagree with such teachings. I believe I understand the rationale behind the Pope's edict, but I do not agree with it. And I feel that I am in a small way entitled to give my opinion on this because I have encountered so many people who murdered other people and were not in the slightest contrite, nor would they ever be. You see, we are not all Christians in this world, and we must understand that.

In recent times, we have experienced the attacks by radical Muslims all over the world. I shudder to think what would have happened if Mohamed Atta and his colleagues had survived their monstrous attack on the Twin Towers, and were incarcerated rather than executed for what they had done. Firstly, they would have been very disappointed, and more important, they would constitute a horrendous danger to the rest of mankind for as long as they lived.

And I dare say I had an interesting experience with a Hindu client of mine who was sentenced to death in Trinidad in the seventies. The day before he was executed, he asked to see me, so I went to the Royal Gaol where I saw him in the condemned cells. We spoke for some time, and I explained that I was quite disappointed because I had composed a Mercy Petition for him and delivered it to the Governor General, only to be informed that he had himself written to the Governor General humbly requesting that he be granted a swift execution. His Excellency thereupon rejected my petition but granted his.

I asked him why he had done that, and this was what he said, "Sir, I am twenty-one years of age and I am a Hindu. I believe that when I leave this world I shall be given the opportunity of elevating myself to a higher form. I therefore am looking forward to that experience. What is more, Sir, is this: I am not used to discipline and to people giving me orders. If I were to remain here in prison, it is a positive that I will kill one or more of these prison officers. Therefore, let me go my way, please!" That man was Moonan Poolool.

So, there you are. Make up your own minds about the death penalty. In passing, I can mention that Dole Chadee, who was executed in 1990, told me three days before his execution that he agreed with the death penalty. But more about him later.

It is said that the death penalty is not a deterrent. I have very serious doubts about that assertion, because my experience tells me it is simply not true. For when Dole Chadee and his colleagues were executed there were very few murders, if any at all, in Trinidad for about six weeks. I thought at the time that if we could span the executions for say, one every week, it would be a good thing. Nowadays, we have no less than seven murders a week in Trinidad, and sometime that figure is as high as twelve.

Trinidad has become a very dangerous place in recent years. Decent folk are afraid to go out after dark, and only the criminals are allowed to have firearms, albeit illegally. The police are no longer trusted by the people for a number of reasons. Firstly, there seems to be complete disdain by them for members of the public and this is clearly seen whenever one has reason to visit a police station. You are met by very angry officers who almost seem to be thinking: "Why the hell are you bothering us at this time?" It is a most disconcerting experience, and it almost tells you that you are not welcome in that Police Station at all.

The public has lost all confidence in the courts because the cases take so long to be heard that many times there is no justice. Witnesses die whilst waiting to give evidence, and quite recently a murder trial started in the Assizes after twenty years. How on earth can that inspire confidence. It is nothing but disgraceful.

Thus, the gangsters are in charge and they know it full well. With no police service and a collapsed court system, why should they really care. Trinidad and Tobago is now considered to be among the ten most dangerous countries in the world.

Sir Henry and Lady Pierre (my In Laws)

CHAPTER 7

1970 – BLACK POWER AND MUTINY

Others have written extensively about these events, so I shall merely mention my own experience. It was the days of Geddes Grainger and the Black Power Movement in Trinidad and Tobago. I think the movement was a good one as it was intended to, and did in fact, drive a dagger into the remnants of colonialism.

Up to that time, there was undoubted rampant discrimination still taking place. For example, it was very difficult for people to gain employment with the Banks unless they were of a certain hue or had family connections, or for a black woman to become Carnival Queen. This was wrong and nobody was prepared to do or even say anything about it, until Geddes, later called Makandal Daaga, arrived and did.

Geddes rallied the people and began marching and protesting, and his movement very nearly overthrew the Government. When I see what is happening with our politics today, I sometimes wonder what would have been the outcome if he had succeeded. He did however make a big impact, because from that time forward, there was a leveling of the playing field in many aspects of life which hitherto was not the case.

At the same time of Geddes' movement, there was the mutiny in Tetron Bay. The soldiers were not satisfied with their leader at the time, Col. Johnson, and for a number of other reasons as well, they mutinied. As a result of both these events, Trinidad and Tobago was thrown into turmoil, about ninety soldiers were arrested and charged for mutiny, while Geddes and about fifty of his followers were arrested and taken by boat to Nelson Island, just off Carenage, where they were incarcerated.

For the next two years I would be involved in these two matters, almost exclusively. A one man tribunal – Mr. Lionel Seemungal, Q.C. – was appointed by the Eric Williams Government to review and recommend on the cases of the fifty citizens held on Nelson Island. The ninety soldiers were charged for mutiny, and a number of military persons from Africa and Malaysia were assembled to try our soldiers. What a mess that turned out to be.

The first court martial was headed by Col. Theophilus Yakubu Danjuma of Nigeria, who was appointed president. With him were four other officers, including Col. Ignatius Achampong of Ghana and Maj. Obitre Gama of Uganda. Thirteen soldiers, including the three senior officers, Lieuts. Lasalle, Barzey and Shah, were put on trial.

I appeared for two of the soldiers, Cpl. Carl Lai Leung and Private Maurice Noray. In my opinion they were the two bravest soldiers of the whole lot, bar none. Even the three officers charged with them showed them respect, and very often I thought that it was a 'damn good thing' the two of them were not in charge on the 21st of April, because the result would have been terribly different. I am certain of that.

Col. Achampong was quite a character and privately accused me of making a joke of the court martial. I responded saying, "Well, it really is a joke, isn't it?" Whereupon he said, "Ah, you are right. In my country we would have shot all of them, because when you make a coup you either succeed or you are dead!" I just smiled and walked away.

But ironically, sometime in 1978 I saw him on the BBC Television news being driven off to his execution by firing squad in Ghana, having been overthrown after ruling Ghana for six years. He himself having gained power by a military coup in 1972. I must say he appeared resigned to his fate, as he had earlier explained to me, and he was smiling and waving to the crowd as he went, standing up in the Land Rover jeep. At least he stood and died for what he believed in.

Lt. Col. Obitre Gama announced that he was leaving the Court Martial after only a few weeks, because he was recalled by his country, Uganda. We later found out that he was summoned back there to take up a high position with the new government led by Idi Amin.

Anyway, the first court martial ended around March of 1971 and nine of thirteen were found guilty as charged and sentenced to various lengthy terms of imprisonment. However, the convictions were overturned by the Court of Appeal in 1972; the court finding that the rules of natural justice were not followed by the court martial, and that the plea of condonation advanced by the soldiers had not even been considered by the court.

The defence of condonation was the contention by the soldiers, or certain of them, that Brig. Serrette, their commanding officer, had promised them that they would be immune from prosecution if they surrendered. As a result of that undertaking, they all agreed to surrender, and in the circumstances it was unfair to charge them. This plea never arose until well into the trial, and it was my dear friend and colleague, Jessel Hannays, who was not involved in the case, but came across that defence of condonation in the course of his readings and brought it, first to my attention, and thereafter to the other counsel in the trial. This he did midway in the trial.

Needless to say, the state appealed the decision of the Court of Appeal, but the Privy Council upheld the decision in July 1972, and all the soldiers were freed.

Dr. Williams was livid about the outcome, and the three Appeal Court Judges were targeted by him thereafter. Mr. Clement Phillips, the most brilliant judge to ever sit in that Court was not promoted to the position of Chief Justice when his turn came. And Mr. Georges and Mr. Fraser were hounded out of office and were forced to seek employment outside of Trinidad.

With respect to the detainees incarcerated, Ewart Thorne and I were the first lawyers allowed on Nelson Island to interview and take instructions from our two respective clients, Syl Lowhar and Otto Patrick, with a view to representing them before the Seemungal Tribunal, which sat in Chaguaramas about six months after the state of emergency was declared.

Ewart Thorne was absolutely brilliant, and I felt honored (and I told him so) to accompany him. We were taken by police launch from Carenage to Nelson Island. It was quite an experience for me to see all the soldiers armed with machine guns guarding these men, some of whom were old and invalid. I was really aghast and saddened by the whole experience, and to make matters worse, I saw my good old friend from England, Adrian Espinet (whom I knew as Junior), sitting there. I must say I felt sympathy for them and I still do.

Whatever may be said about the Black Power movement it was responsible for serious progress in our country. Black consciousness became a reality; the dashiki and dreadlocks came to be fully accepted. And many persons took names from their ancestors and were proud to do so. Trinidad changed for the better. What is more, very many of the persons who were incarcerated in Nelson Island were brilliant and really had Trinidad at heart

.

Lowhar's case was heard first, and he was released. Shortly after, my client Otto Patrick was also released. They had spent many months on the island and were very happy to go home.

Thereafter, the cases were all heard and one by one they were freed. The sedition charges were dropped by the Government, and people were allowed to go back to living their usual lives.

Looking back on the events of 1970, I am of the view that it was a most serious period in our history for many reasons. The most important of them was that the people who protested believed, and with justification, that colonialism had not really ended, but instead had become colonialism by privileged locals and commercial institutions. And they were absolutely right.

Jessel Hannays (my Learned and best friend)

CHAPTER 8

MY BROTHER IS KILLED IN A PLANE ACCIDENT

My younger brother Frederick, whom we all called "Ricky" was a wonderful character, always making fun of life. He was the youngest of my siblings, and at age nineteen became a pilot. He joined Carib West Airlines, a freight flying company that was based in Barbados in early 1971, and he was very happy working for them.

On the afternoon of Thursday September 9th 1971, Ricky was at home in Cascade where he lived with our mother. He was on five days leave, having worked continuously for the previous week. However, one of his colleagues, another Trinidadian pilot working for Carib West, telephoned and asked Ricky to do a flight to Guadeloupe that evening for him, because he had a date with a young lady which he wished to keep. Ricky absolutely refused saying he was exhausted and needed the break. But he persisted and called back at least three more times until Ricky relented.

At about 8 pm that evening, the Carib West DC3 aircraft, 8P-AAC, left Piarco Airport bound for Pointe-à-Pitre – Le Raizet Airport – in Guadeloupe. On board were Capt. Bob Anthony, a US citizen, and first officer Ricky De Lima. The cargo comprised five thousand chicks in cases, and a boat engine that weighed about 2000 lbs. At about 11 o'clock that night, the aircraft crashed into the Grand Soufriere mountain in the Basse-Terre region in Guadaloupe.

It took all of three days to locate the wreckage, and a number of our close friends (Colin Laird, Brian Claxton and George Cabral among them) accompanied me to Guadeloupe the day after the crash, and we walked 5500 feet up the mountain in search of the aircraft.

At about 3 pm on Sunday the 12th, we found the wreckage, and both Bob and Ricky were lying dead next to it. Together with the gendarmes, (the French military), we brought the two bodies down the mountain. Bob's body was returned to his family in the USA, and I accompanied Ricky's back to Trinidad the same night.

I had the privilege of hearing the official air traffic control tape dealing with the case, and this is what actually happened. Carib West was on its final approach having been given permission to land by the Pointe-a-Pitre tower. Then an Air France jet airliner with more than one hundred persons aboard announced that it was immediately behind Carib West, and there was a great deal of French being spoken between the air traffic controller in the tower and the Air France plane, when Ricky announces on the intercom that Carib West would give way to the Air France flight, and that they would turn left.

Air France then lands, whereupon the air traffic controller calls for Carib West to give its position. Ricky is heard responding and then the air traffic controller frantically shouts, "No, no, no, Carib West! The mountain!" Then Ricky is heard saying, "Carib West ascending, going through 3,000 feet." Then there is the sound of a thud and then, silence.

Ricky's death had an everlasting impact on our dear mother,

from which I don't think she ever recovered. He was not only her last child, but was also her companion in her house in Cascade.

He was also engaged to be married to a lovely girl from Barbados, Donna Scott, at whose request, I took her ring off his finger on the mountain and returned it to her. Donna is still alive, happily married, and lives in Barbados.

Sometime later we were informed by Carib West that the air controller had been criminally charged for negligence and was sent to Paris to stand trial. That really was of little or no interest to us because we regarded it a tragic accident which nobody could have predicted.

My brother Ricky

CHAPTER 9

THE 1970's & RANDOLPH BURROUGHS

To my mind, the seventies were one of the most frightening periods in Trinidad and Tobago. Shortly after the black power movement and the mutiny were put down by the Williams government, Randolph Burroughs was allowed full leeway to do as he pleased with crime and persons he suspected of committing crime in the country. Into being came the 'Flying Squad', a band of policemen of the most dubious character who were virtually a law unto themselves, and who had absolutely no compunction in letting the public know that.

The Flying Squad had the blessing of Dr. Williams, and one of its first missions was to deal with NUFF (the National Union of Freedom Fighters) which it did by arresting and murdering many innocent people. I recall a young policeman coming to me for advice. He said that he was transferred to the Flying Squad, and that on a particular raid made by Burroughs and his men, the police fired more than one thousand rounds into a wooden house in which there were three suspects – even though the suspects wanted to surrender and had in fact raised a white flag to indicate that.

All three were shot dead, and afterwards Burroughs called all his men together and walked from one to the other feeling the barrels of their weapons to ascertain that they had all been fired. In the case of my client, Burroughs found that the barrel was not hot enough and he appeared angry with him.

I advised him to request a transfer which he did successfully; otherwise, he was prepared to resign and seek other employment. Today he is a senior officer in the Trinidad and Tobago Police Service.

In my view, this was when police, framing members of the public with crimes, really began with a bang. And if you took the time to investigate it, you would find that Burroughs or one or more of his men were involved.

Mr. Procope and I first became aware of this in the case of a bookmaker and his girlfriend, whose apartment in Alagonda Flats, St. Anns was raided by Burroughs and his men, and the couple was charged for possession of cocaine and ammunition.

The police alleged that they found the items in a pouf in the drawing room, but one of them forgot the story and testified that they found it in the toilet bowl. The case was dismissed, but the seriousness of it really dawned thereafter when we began encountering that type of evidence far more frequently, including in capital cases, as in the case of Kissoon Ramnannan.

CHAPTER 10

THEY HANG AN INNOCENT MAN

At about 7:45 pm on Saturday the 12th of September 1970, at the corner of Delhi and Agra Streets in St. James, Inspector Kenneth Cooke was shot twice in the chest. He was visiting his elderly mother who lived nearby and noticed three men liming[3] around his parked car. He approached them and one of them shot him. They ran and jumped into a car nearby and sped away. As a result of the gunshots, the Inspector died on the spot within seconds.

This is a most important case, because it shows clearly how and when some of our Trinidad police not only became corrupt, but became dangerously corrupt.

Inspector Ken Cooke was a very good and popular man. He was a sportsman and also was in charge of the equestrian division of the police service and taught many persons, including the Prime Minister's daughter Erica, horseback riding. Trinidad was shocked and Randolph Burroughs immediately went into action. He called a meeting of the Flying Squad and informed them that this was unacceptable, and it was imperative that an arrest be made as soon as possible.

---

3. A Trinidadian term for relaxed chatting with friends or acquaintances.

Kissoon Ramnannan was a known car thief who lived in Suchit Trace, Penal. Some days after Insp. Cooke's murder, Ramnannan bought a motor car from one Berner Francis, a straightener and painter, who owned a small garage in California. He paid one thousand dollars for it, but unbeknown to him, this car was the one which was seen speeding away from the murder scene in St James. The police arrested Ramnannan when he was found driving the said motor car, and despite his protests of innocence, his alibi that he was in Biche on the night of the incident was never investigated, and he was charged for the Ken Cooke murder.

The prosecution relied primarily on the evidence of two witnesses, Alfredo Francis and Michael Lal, both of whom testified that they were present on the scene of the crime at the time, and witnessed the accused shoot Inspector Cooke. They both gave evidence that not only did they see Ramnannan at the scene, but they independently picked him out at Identification Parades separately conducted by Supt. Jeremiah Gordon at Police Headquarters in Port of Spain on Monday 12th of October 1970.

The case was first tried in the Port of Spain Assizes, presided over by Justice Garvin Scott in June 1971. Dr. Aeneas Wills appeared for the defence and the jury failed to agree on a verdict. Consequently, the matter was adjourned to the very next Assizes, and restarted before Justice John Braithwaite on the 21st July 1971. This time the accused did not have the services of Dr. Wills because he was otherwise engaged. Instead, he was represented by Mr. Clyde Creville. On the 27th of July 1970, the jury returned a verdict of guilty of murder and he was sentenced to death by hanging.

Kissoon Ramnannan appealed to the Court of Appeal, and on the 20th of December 1971 the Court of Appeal comprising Justices Fraser, De la Bastide and Georges dismissed the appeal and affirmed the conviction and sentence.

In October 1972, a Petition for Special Leave to Appeal as a poor person was presented to the Privy Council in London, UK on his behalf, but this too was refused.

Thereafter, a Petition was presented to the Mercy Committee not asking for a reprieve or pardon, but asking it to investigate the case because he was innocent. This too was denied. My learned friend Selwyn Mohammed, a probation officer at the time, submitted a report and recommended mercy, which was also refused.

Kissoon Ramnannan was hanged at the Royal Gaol on Tuesday the 18th of September 1973.

I first met Kissoon Ramnannan in the condemned cells in early 1972. During one of my visits to the gaol to meet with the soldiers whom I was representing, Raffique Shah and Rex Lasalle both told me about him and asked me to visit him and hear what he had to say. They were both very impressed with him and were convinced that he was innocent.

So very soon after, I arranged to see Ramnannan. He not only told me that he was innocent of the murder, but also gave me the names of the three men he said committed the murder. Of the three, I knew two and it just so happened that at that time, one was in prison awaiting trial and was making arrangements to have his family retain me for his case. So, I summoned him to the barristers' room and confronted him with what Ramnannan had told me. He stared at me for about a minute without saying a word. He then made sure the guard standing nearby couldn't hear him and he said, "Sir, it is true. I was there but I was not the one who shot the police officer, that was not me! And Sir, Ramnannan is telling the truth, he was not there." He then told me the name of the man who actually shot the Inspector and the name of the third man.

I said to him, "You can't allow Ramnannan to die for a crime he did not commit. Give me an affidavit telling the truth and I promise I shall represent you free of charge and I'll do my best to see that you are all right." He looked at me and said, "Mr. De Lima, you know how long the police looking to get me? I would be as good as dead if I did that. I will not do it!"

I got up and left the prison. What is more, he retained another lawyer to do his case and I never saw him again. I do know however that he and the other one whom I knew, both migrated to the USA.

Prison culture is a very real thing. If a man is in prison innocently, believe me, a lot of the other prisoners know. And many of the prison officers know as well, because they live among the prisoners and they are made aware of what is what. So that when Ramnannan was executed, many of the prison officers were upset because they very well knew what had gone down.

I was now convinced of the innocence of Kissoon Ramnannan, but I really did not know what I could do to help him. I couldn't reveal what the prisoner had told me because of the attorney-client privilege rule. I was well and truly stumped.

The Privy Council refused his petition in late 1972, and sometime in February 1973, a date was fixed for his execution. I was resolved to try to do something to save this man's life.

I knew that Mr. Raymond Dabadie, who was the Secretary of the Trinidad Turf Club, was a member of the Mercy Committee, so I went to his home and told him what I knew about the case. The next day he called me and said that he was able to have the execution adjourned, so that a full inquiry into the circumstances of the case could be had. I was relieved and I went to the Prison and told Ramnannan, who broke down in tears of joy. I was so happy and I thanked Almighty God. I was convinced that justice would be done and that Kissoon would be able to go home one day.

In those days I was quite naïve, always thinking that good always prevails over evil, etc. I always walked brave because of my faith.

I heard nothing more about this case until about a week before the 18th of September 1973. I was sitting at my desk in 11 St Vincent Street when the phone rang and it was Mr. Dabadie. He said, "Vernon, I'm sorry to tell you that Ramnannan will be executed next Monday the 18th." The Investigators said their inquiry revealed no new information. I remember asking him who were the Investigators, and he said, "The same officers who testified at the trial." All I said then was, "My God. No!"

The day before Kissoon Ramnannan was executed, I went to the Prison to see him. I sat there outside his cell when he said to me, "Mr. De Lima. I want to thank you for everything you did for me." I replied, "But Kissoon, I really did nothing. We tried but we didn't succeed. I'm sorry."

He said, "Promise me Sir, that if you ever get the opportunity to establish my innocence, you will do it." I agreed.

And then he said this, "I know you never charged me any money. But I am going to pay you for all you tried to do for me. Here is how. Tomorrow morning, at 7 am when I stand before Almighty God, I will put in a word for you!" I choked and the two prison officers near me began to cry. It was the nicest thing anyone ever said to me. I got up, said goodbye, and left.

The next day, at about 8 am, I went to the Prison to see another client and as I walked in, I saw the hearse in the courtyard. As I was walking across the yard to the Supervisor's office, His Grace the Archbishop Anthony Pantin was coming down the stairs and he was clapping his hands and calling me. I stopped and he came up to me and said, "Vernon, they hanged an innocent man here just now!" I replied, "But father, didn't you know that? Everybody knew he was innocent!" Thereupon he invited me to come to Archbishop's house to have a cup of tea (or coffee) with him, and I agreed.

After seeing my client, I went to Archbishop's House where Fr. Pantin explained that Kissoon had converted to Catholicism a few months before, and had requested as his last wish that he, Pantin, be present at his execution. His Grace said he couldn't refuse, and so he went to the cell at about 6:30 am and prayed with him. At 7 am, just before the hood was placed over his head, he said to the Archbishop, "Father, thank you for being here with me. As the last thing I say on this earth, and I ask you to bear witness. They are executing me for something I know nothing about." He was then hanged. It was Tuesday the 18th of September 1973.

I was devastated. But I had to go on, as Mr. O'Reilly had said years before. However, it would not be long before I would be able to keep my promise to Kissoon.

On the 26th of July 1974, during the course of a presentation I was doing on the matter of Identification Parades at a Law Conference in Chaguaramas, I mentioned that sometimes mistakes could be made in matters of identification. When the question time arrived, a member asked, "Mr. De Lima, do you know of any case where a person suffered because of mistaken identification?" I said yes, and that it was the case of Kissoon Ramnannan who was executed even though he was innocent. Of course, this caused an uproar, and shortly after the meeting was adjourned to two days hence.

The very next day, a policeman by the name of Rudolph Regis (aka 'Scorpion') came to my Chambers to speak about the Ramnannan case. He said he had had a sleepless night, and that he had spoken with his wife who told him to come to me and tell me what happened.

He told me that he heard on the radio and read in today's

paper what I said at Chaguaramas the day before, and that I was right because the police did frame Ramnannan, who was totally innocent. He said that he and another policeman named Villafarna were detailed in the charge room of CID in Port of Spain on the morning that Ramnannan was brought in and handcuffed to a bench. It was about 4 am when the prisoner arrived. At about 6 am, whilst Ramnannan was asleep, the police brought two men, Alfred Francis and Michael Lal, and had them have a good and long look at Ramnannan whilst he was lying asleep there, and later, at about 10 am, the Identification Parade was held, whereupon Kissoon was identified by both Alfred Francis and Michael Lal.

I asked him to give me a written statement and he said, "Mr. De Lima I am a policeman. This is the job I have."

Not long after this, Regis fell ill, and I tried to see him to get an affidavit, but he refused and he died.

I found out that ASP Villafarna lived in Santa Cruz, and I went in search of him. I found him and was able to speak with him about the case. He was dying of cancer and looked very gaunt. He admitted to me that he knew Ramnannan was innocent, but he too refused to give me a written statement. He died shortly after I spoke with him.

As I said earlier, this case shows how dangerous the police had become in the seventies. This was not a case of mistaken identification, which I thought it may have been when I presented the paper on I.D. parades in Chaguaramas. Instead, it was a massive conspiracy by many senior police officers to murder Kissoon Ramnannan by unlawfully hanging him. It was a demonic plot that took several years, including the investigation requested by the Mercy Committee. From that time onwards, I never trusted the police in Trinidad and Tobago because I was well aware that many of them whom I knew were associated with Ramnannan's case continued to be in the Service, and indeed had been promoted to higher positions since that time. What is more, I would have to interact with some of them in the future. It also became clear to me why neither Regis nor Villafarna were prepared to go public with their information. We were now in frightening times.

CHAPTER 11

MICHAEL De FREITAS, aka ABDUL MALIK

This is one of the most interesting cases I appeared in over the fifty years I practiced.

Michael De Freitas was born in Trinidad in 1933 to Iona Brown, a Bajan woman, and her common law husband called De Freitas. They lived together in a small house in McCarthy Lane, Belmont until he was four. His father De Freitas then left their home and migrated to St. Kitts, where he lived out the rest of his life.

Iona raised her son as best she could, and when he was eighteen he became a seaman and sailed away, working on various boats all over the world, until he eventually settled in England in or around 1957. There he married a Guyanese woman, Desiree, and they had four children.

In England, he got into trouble with the law on more than one occasion. He took the name Michael X, and then later Michael Abdul Malik, and he mixed with high society folk such as Princess Margaret and her husband, Lord Anthony Snowden, John Lennon and Yoko Ono, and Lord David Pitt. His friends in the USA included Mohammed Ali, Martin Luther King, Malcolm X, and Dick Gregory. In fact, Lennon, Ono, Ali and

Gregory all visited Trinidad at different times to visit with Malik, and Lennon and Yoko stayed at Malik's home when they came.

I first met Malik in September of 1972. His trial for the murder of Joseph Skeritt had just finished, and he was in the condemned cell awaiting his execution. I was visited by his wife Desiree at my Chambers in Port of Spain, and she requested that I pay him a visit. The following day I went to the Royal Gaol where we spoke, and he asked me to represent him in his appeal. The matter of my fee was discussed and agreed. I was now officially his lawyer.

I immediately notified the Court of Appeal in Trinidad, and a few days later met with Sir Issac Hyatali, C.J. in his Chambers, where we discussed the matter of the timing of the appeal. I requested at least six months and we agreed that an appropriate time would be the end of March 1973.

This was sufficient time for me, and I informed Malik accordingly. He was pleased with the arrangement. I should add that Sir Issac also informed me that he had instructed the Court of Appeal's librarians that I should be accorded all assistance should the need arise in locating any authority.

Before I presented the appeal, I was inundated with calls from all sorts of persons from England and the United States who were friends of Malik, and wanted to assist him in any way they could. These included lawyers as well. A Lord Gifford, whom I mistakenly called "Lord Kitchener" in a telephone conversation (needless to say he was furious with me), wanted to come to Trinidad to sit with me during the appeal. Then there was Mr. William Kunstler, a New York attorney, who told me that John Lennon had paid him to come to Trinidad to assist, and then Mr. Lennox Hinds of the National Conference of Black Lawyers in New York. It was unreal. These folks just popped up from all over. I thanked them very much for their concern but assured them that I was all right and did not need their assistance.

I spent the next ten weeks or so studying the brief. I had the assistance of my dear friend Jessel Hannays, and many a night we would sit on the porch of my home in St Augustine discussing and turning the whole case over and over. Jessel and I always loved doing appeals because they involved law primarily. Questions of fact are decided by the jury, and there is not very much the appeal lawyer is able to complain about there. But questions of law, that's another matter. Those are always regarded as very serious, and unless the Court of Appeal is able to conclude that notwithstanding the mistake in law that took place, the Court is of the opinion that no miscarriage of justice occurred, which the court rarely says, the appeal would be allowed and the sentence quashed.

In the course of our studies we came across just such a matter of law and it was this:

In the course of the trial, there was a meeting of all the lawyers in the Judge's Chambers during a lunch break. At this meeting, the lawyers requested that some editing be done to Abbott's statement, which was in fact, a confession, which the Attorney General intended to tender in evidence at some later stage. They referred the Judge to authorities and he decided that he had the authority to edit. So the statement was edited by the lawyers and the new statement was signed, not by Abbott but by the trial Judge. The meeting then ended. All this took 85 minutes and none of the accused were present. Sometime later, the complainant, Insp. Ignatius Mc Phillip, took the witness stand. He was asked if he took a statement from Abbott and he answered in the affirmative. Thereupon he identified the original statement, and it was marked as an exhibit but not read to the court. Immediately thereafter, the Attorney General tendered the abridged statement that was agreed to in the Judge's Chambers at the lunchtime meeting. This was then admitted and read to the jury as evidence of the statement given by Abbott.

I therefore filed only one ground of appeal, which I labelled ground 1(a) and 1(b):

> "The learned trial Judge was wrong in law when he conducted part of the trial of the appellant in the absence of:
>
> 1(a) The Appellant himself and
> 1(b) The Public
>
> to wit, when he edited or allowed to be edited or altered or allowed to be altered, the confession of the co-accused Stanley Abbott at a sitting held in his Chambers on the 2nd of August, 1972, at which neither the Appellant nor the other accused nor the Public was present, as a consequence whereof, the said trial was and is a nullity."

I presented my arguments to the Court of Appeal on Monday the 26th of March 1973 and I submitted, among other things, that the strange proceedings that had taken place in the Judge's Chambers amounted to a 'Cancer of Irregularity' that nullified the trial.

The Court delivered its decision three weeks later on the 17th of April 1973.

The Court said, "In our view, the proceedings in the Judge's chambers constituted no more than an informal meeting, at which the Judge, on the invitation of counsel, promoted an agreement to exclude, on humanitarian and merciful grounds and not on evidential or legal grounds, passages in Abbott's statement which were not evidence against Malik, but which were thought likely, notwithstanding that fact, to prejudice the minds of members of the jury against him. This ground is therefore rejected."

That was that. I did not agree with the court and I have always felt that had the appellant been anybody other than Abdul Malik, the result would have been different.

There are a few things about this case I feel I should speak about. Firstly, the trial judge, Mr. Evan Rees, was my personal friend. He was not only my friend, but he was a good, honest and God-fearing man, who always bent over backward to do justice. We remained friends to the day he died, and I always remember him in my prayers. He was fearless but fair.

Secondly, I had the feeling that my client had rubbed a lot of people the wrong way. I felt that there were more people who were afraid of him than liked him.

Thirdly, this case brought home to me vividly, that rich and famous people are not necessarily good people, and that in life you've got to be very careful who you trust. It is a very difficult mission but I will give you, the reader, a rule that I learned many years ago from a wise man which I found to be a good rule: "WHEN IN DOUBT, SAY NO!" And that means ANY doubt, about anybody or anything. It has served me well and I advise you, you would do well to remember it.

Malik appealed to the Privy Council in November 1973, and I understand that the application took no more than twenty minutes. The English Privy Council Judges knew who he was, and they wanted to have no part of him.

After the appeal in Trinidad, I never saw him again. I kept in touch with Mr. Conrad Sanguinette who was his solicitor, who kept me informed about his case.

Malik was hanged at the Royal Gaol in Port of Spain on Friday the 16th of May 1975. It was the first time that anyone was hanged on a day other than a Tuesday in Trinidad.

Abdul Malik, Muhammad Ali and Dr. Eric Williams

CHAPTER 12

THE AMERICAN KID I CALLED 'BILLY BOY'

He was only seventeen years old when he was caught by the police with cocaine in a room at the Normandie Hotel, St. Anns, in Port of Spain, in the company of a notorious drug dealer of the day named Winston Bruce, alias 'Dr. Rat.'

Billy Boy appeared the following day before the Magistrate and pleaded guilty. He was sentenced to two years hard labor. Dr. Rat pleaded not guilty, was given bail and later was found not guilty, because he contended that Billy Boy was the one who had the drugs and had pleaded guilty. Made sense, so the magistrate dismissed the case against him.

Shortly after he was sentenced, the US Embassy contacted me and the officer there asked if I would do the appeal and I agreed.

I went to Golden Grove Prison and when Billy Boy was brought in to the Barristers' room, I was shocked by his appearance. He was about six feet tall and very gaunt and pale white. Both his arms were discolored with needle tracks and his eyes were sunken. I asked him why he took drugs, and this is what he said, "Sir, my father is a very wealthy man. He owns one of the biggest chain stores in the USA. I am his eldest child and I have

77

a sister who is aged eight. I would like to have a profession of my choice, but my father insists that I come into his business. Every time he asks me what I want to do and I respond, he would simply say, "Boy, don't be an ass, we have fifty of those working for us." Then he added, "He's killed my spirit, Sir, so I really don't care anymore."

I looked at this young, pathetic boy and felt so sorry for him.

Six weeks later, the appeal came on. The day before the hearing, a privately-owned Learjet arrived at Piarco Airport with three American lawyers on board. They came to attend the hearing of Billy Boy's appeal.

I addressed the Court, which was presided over by the Chief Justice Sir Issac Hyatali, and explained what I knew about this young man and pleaded for leniency. I also explained that the three gentlemen who were seated in the public gallery were US attorneys who had come to Trinidad at the request of Billy Boy's father and that there was a plane waiting at Piarco to take Billy Boy out of Trinidad that same day if the Court was disposed to give him such opportunity.

Sir Issac immediately invited the three lawyers to sit at the Bar table, and the Court adjourned for fifteen minutes. When it resumed, Sir Issac asked me if I could guarantee the Court if they released Billy Boy that he would be out of Trinidad that day. I said I could, and the Court made the order. He was taken by the prison van from Golden Grove Prison to Piarco Airport where he boarded the Learjet and left at 3:30 pm that day for the United States. I was very pleased that he was given this chance, and I told him so at Piarco before he left.

About two weeks later, I received a telephone call from one of the American lawyers who had come to Trinidad, and he told me that he was saddened to inform me that Billy Boy was dead because he was shot by the FBI in a hotel room in New York.

I often remember this case because it taught me an important lesson, that a young man or woman must be encouraged to do a profession that he or she wants and not what the parents want, and that all the money in the world should not be allowed to influence this principle. The old, famous calypsonian, Lord Pretender sang: "Blessed is the child that has his own shilling." And he was right! I always thought Pretender was a prophet, and when he sang "Never, never worry" I was certain of it.

CHAPTER 13

'COCK TO FIGHT' AND JOHNNY O'

On Sunday 4th of May 1975, about three hundred people, including ex-government Minister Johnny O'Halloran were arrested by the police in San Raphael, Arima, and charged under the Summary Offences Ordinance for cockfighting.

Cockfighting has been going on in Trinidad for over two hundred years. In fact, the island was under Spanish rule for more than three hundred years, and cockfighting was then, and still is, a huge sport in Spain.

One merely has to consider the names of some of the persons who have over the years been known to promote the sport to get my drift: Rivas, Navarro, Lourenco, De Lima, Gonzales, Castillo, Guzman, Pacheco, Fortune, Rojas, Farfan. And many of the names of places in Trinidad are a strong reminder of our Spanish past: viz., Port of Spain, San Raphael, Arima, Sangre Grande, Las Cuevas, Cumana, Sangre Chicito, Maraval, Santa Margarita, Cumoto, Los Gordos, Brasso Seco, etc.

Over the years, the French influence came into the sport as well. For example, many of the attacks that one cock will launch against the other is described by the crowd in French; e.g.,

'Mussuyel' is a cutting blow to the throat, 'Pattisec' is a passing shot to the body, and 'Tumbauo' is a knock-out or lethal shot which sometimes ended in sudden death.

The cocks have their own personalities as well, and are given names by the fans according to their ability. The absolute champion cock of Trinidad was called 'Carajo,' which means 'prick' in Spanish. He was a runt of a bird that was found running around a Venezuelian boat that came to Port of Spain to deliver dry goods in the 60's. One of the Navarro brothers, Tonio, asked the Capitan if he could have the bird and he agreed. Carajo won twenty-one battles, never lost one and ended up as a stud bird whose eggs were sought-after – even by people from Venezuela. Another champion bird was called 'Wiltshire the Butcher'. I am told he was a great fighter who demolished his rivals within the first minute of his fights. He was owned by the famous and popular Fedo De Gannes of Diego Martin.

I have absolutely no doubt that cockfighting is part of our culture and heritage in Trinidad. Just a few miles away in neighboring Venezuela, it is legal. The French allow it as well. Martinique and Guadaloupe are big into cockfighting, which is legal there.

I represented all the persons who were charged at San Raphael when they appeared in the Arima Magistrates' Court on the following day, Monday the 5th, and they pleaded not guilty. Our intention was to present the case for the defence, so as to establish that the sport was not cruel. We did that and called as our expert witness, Dr. Steve Bennett, a very well-recognized and respected veterinarian, who testified that the cocks were *ferae naturae*, which means wild by nature and incapable of being tamed.

As expected, we lost the case before the magistrate, and we proceeded to the Court of Appeal. There we lost again. There is no doubt that the sport is illegal in Trinidad and that the only way forward for cockfighters is to move to have the law repealed.

It really is a shame though. The people who fight cocks are in the majority middle class and/or poor people who can afford to breed their own birds from eggs probably given to them. They will never be able to own a racehorse or a speedboat or a racing car, or go to a casino and spend a thousand dollars. They proudly fight their birds for stakes of two, three or four hundred dollars. They keep to themselves and one rarely hears of crime taking place in the "gayelle" (the arena in the bush) where the cockfights are held. Whenever the matter of legalizing it comes up, there is a hue and cry from the TSPCA which is seldom otherwise ever heard from.

I am certain that one day not too far off, cockfighting will be legalized in Trinidad. Just like marijuana has been. And maybe when that happens, the annual classic event may be called 'The O'Halloran Cup' or 'The Kong Trophy'. Quien sabe?

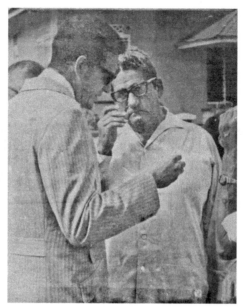

John O'Halloran and me. Outside the Cock fight Court in Arima.

The Giant – Dr. Steve Bennett

CHAPTER 14

LOUIS GONZALEZ, aka 'PILOT'

At about 10:30 pm on the night of 28th of October 1977, Louis Gonzalez, a BWIA pilot, was dropped to his home at Scott Bushe Street, Corbeaux Town, by a taxi from Piarco, having just arrived from the USA where he completed courses for his employment. He was greeted by his wife and his mother. He had been away for ten days and was very tired but glad to be home.

About fifteen minutes after he arrived, there started loud guitar and quatro music with persons singing loudly in the street. His mother explained that a number of Venezuelan girls had recently moved into the house across the road, and that the Venezuelan male students had been coming there every night for the past week and playing their quatros and singing aloud, making it impossible for the neighbors to sleep, and that she had complained to them but they didn't take her on.

The noise continued for about another hour, after which Louis got out of his bed and picked up a starting pistol he had in his room for protection and went to his front gate and shouted: "For God's sake, stop this noise now. I can't sleep and neither can anyone in my home!"

Immediately, five Venezuelan men ran across the road towards him and he retreated up his steps. Two of the Venezuelans entered his property and one of them had a firearm and fired a shot at him, whereupon he fired off his starting pistol and ran back inside his house. Shortly after, the police were called. The next day, Louis was arrested and charged for shooting one of the Venezuelans and possessing an unlicensed firearm and ammunition...'the whole nine yards'. The Venezuelan had received superficial burns to his hand and face.

I was retained by Louis shortly after the incident and he told me right away what had happened. As a result, I wasn't in the least worried about him because his instructions clearly revealed self defence. The Venezuelans had attacked him in his property and with a gun. I made sure that he gave a written statement to the police detailing all that had happened. In fact, he gave them the same statement he gave to me.

Louis's case came on for trial at the Port of Spain Assizes before Justice Lennox Deyalsingh (his very first case as a new judge) on the 30th March 1979, and the prosecution called only one Venezuelan witness, the one who suffered the burns. I was told by counsel for the prosecution. Mr. Ranjie Dolsingh, that the State would be calling no other witness of the event. I protested but could do no more. What is more, the State had Louis' statement which gave the whole defence, but when he gave evidence they put it to him that his defence was a total fabrication to save himself, and that he had unlawfully attacked the student who was unarmed at the time. It was just unbelievable, but that is what occurred.

The jury returned after two hours with a verdict of guilty and Louis was sentenced to four years imprisonment with hard labor. His mother Elena almost died of shock, and his Canadian wife left for Canada right away with their year-old child and never returned. His whole life was destroyed.

I was stunned by what had happened. Louis lost all hope in our judicial system and refused to appeal. He gave up and settled down in Golden Grove Prison to doing what he was told to do and making handicraft artifacts and the like. He was quite a hit with the other prisoners who called him 'Pilot' and the prison officers also loved him.

The people of Corbeaux Town knew Louis well and knew what he was and was not capable of, and so they rallied for him; they included Jackie Williams, Gerry Hadeed, Ming Johnson, Trevor Smith, Louis Delmas and George Gonzalez and many others. They presented a Petition of more than 5,000 persons for clemency to the President.

On the 31st of August 1980, His Excellency President Ellis Clarke pardoned Louis Gonzalez and he walked out of the Prison a free man. One year later, his Corbeaux Town friends had a dinner at Ling Nam restaurant to celebrate his presidential pardon.

But the forces had conspired against him, poor fellow. His wife, a Canadian, had left with their now two-year-old daughter and returned to Canada. He would never see them again.

Louis waited a whole year and did whatever had to be done to get back his license to fly. He renewed his Airline Transport Pilot's License and then applied to BWIA for reinstatement. In support of his application, the Chairman of TTALPA, the Pilots Association, wrote to Mr. I. Bertrand, the Managing Director of BWIA, recommending Louis' reinstatement.

On the 21st January 1982, Bertrand wrote to Louis stating that BWIA was not employing at that time but would consider him in the future if and when the time came. A total sham. Here was a case of a man who was pardoned and now needed employment. A man who had worked for BWIA for three years before.

I thought then, and I still think now, that the reason Louis Gonzalez was refused re-employment in BWIA was the airline strike that took place in 1978. That was a most distasteful event, and ended with most of our good pilots leaving Trinidad for Singapore. The BWIA pilots were known to be the best in the world, and to see that we lost all those good pilots for the reasons we did is painful. The Government of the day was not only unfair to the pilots, but the way it dealt with the situation traumatized the whole nation. It certainly killed BWIA, and today that airline is no more, sorry to say.

Anyway, Louis was refused reinstatement by BWIA, so he went to Tobago where he owned a condominium and began working, packaging and freezing fresh fish and lobster, which he then transported to Trinidad. He really had a good product and even Hi Lo and Artie's carried Louis' fish. Just like he was in prison, he was very popular with all the fisherfolk of Tobago; they loved him and kept him supplied with fish, lobster and conch so that he was able to make a comfortable living.

Many years later, on the 10th of November 1989, ex-Inspector Oscar King, who was a Police Interpreter, gave evidence on day 33 of the La Tinta Inquiry. In the course of his evidence, he said he knew that Louis Gonzalez was innocent, and that he, King, was the official Police Interpreter at the time, and that shortly after the incident at Scott Bushe Street, he was requested by Asst. Commissioner of Crime, Gordon Waterman, to interview and take statements from the two Venezuelan students, and that when he did so, they admitted to him that one of them was armed with a gun and entered Louis' yard and fired a shot at Louis causing him to return fire.

He further said that he had tendered the statements to Waterman so that he was shocked and saddened to read in the papers that Louis was convicted.

He went on further to say that he had expected that in view

of the statements he had taken, he would have been called by the State as a witness. His actual words were: "My God. I am so sorry. That man was innocent. He lost his job at BWIA. I wanted to give evidence real bad!"

The day after Inspector King gave his evidence, Louis telephoned me from Tobago and he was sobbing as he said, "Vernon, you remember I told you that that was what happened? Well now at least people will know I was not lying." And then everybody knew he was not.

The civil lawyers explained to Louis that he could sue the State and in all probability he would be awarded substantial damages. He would hear nothing of it. He said he didn't ever want to enter another court in Trinidad and Tobago and just wanted to be left alone. He continued living in Tobago and selling his fish until he died of cancer on the 21st of January 2002 at Mt. Hope Hospital.

I often think about Louis, and I consider it a privilege to have known him. I think he made me be a better person.

I once wrote this about him: "Louis Gonzalez did not get a fair shake in life – I think. But what I am certain of is that he has gone to a place where he can no longer be wronged and where he will receive full and fair disclosure upon his trial. And there will be no withholding of exculpatory evidence in that place."

May he rest in peace…my friend and client, Louis Gonzalez.

My friend and client,
Louis Gonzalez and his mother Elena.

CHAPTER 15

LA TINTA – WHAT REALLY HAPPENED

La Tinta is a beautiful beach on the western side of Chacachacare Island, commonly called 'Chac' which belongs to Trinidad, and is situated about ten miles west of Port of Spain. The island is horseshoe shaped and comprises some 900 acres and was originally named by Christopher Columbus 'El Caracol', which means 'the Snail'. The Spaniards grew cotton on the island, and later it became a prominent whaling station. The beach is called La Tinta, which is Spanish for 'ink', because the sand there is black.

I have often wondered why it is that 'Chac' was never spruced up and made into a tourist paradise. It is a beautiful island with a few beaches which are exquisite. And the fishing, both trolling and banking near and around the island, is very good. Donald Trump visited 'Chac' in 1999 during the Miss Universe contest that was held in Trinidad, and announced he would build a Hotel there, but it seems that that idea was shelved.

In or around 1922, Chacachacare was commissioned as an asylum for persons afflicted with leprosy (Hansen's disease), and it was run by the sisters of the French Dominican Order. In those days, the illness was considered very contagious. The leprosarium was closed down in 1984 and other than some folks who picnic on a long weekend, there is very little that goes on there. I am grateful to my dear friend Sister Marie Therese Retout, who worked for many years in the Royal Gaol in Port of Spain, for the many works she compiled about 'Chac', and to which I make reference. She is, and always was, a person dedicated to the truth and humanity, and Jennifer and I consider it a blessing from Almighty God to have known her.

THE BUST

At about 5 pm on the afternoon of Tuesday the 24th of February 1987, a party of policemen comprising about sixteen officers belonging to the Narcotic Squad, left the Port of Spain CID, boarded a hired pirogue piloted by former Lance Corporal Lincoln Charles, in Chaguaramas, and headed to Chacachacare, on a mission they referred to as a 'Buy and Bust'. One of the policemen, Cpl. Hugh Bernard, carried with him a briefcase containing $50,000.00 in US currency and $30,000.00 TT which he had taken from the police vault in CID, where it had been lodged as a court exhibit in an unconnected matter.

The officers on this mission were: Sgt. Milton Sebro, Cpl. Akim Treia, Cpl. Alfred Sealey, Cpl. Hugh Bernard, P.C. Roger Black, Cpl. Reynold Craig, P.C. John Kennedy, P.C. Kurt Campo, P.C. Phillip Salvary, P.C. Fournellier, P.C. Abraham, P.C. Delfish, P.C. Austin, P.C. Narcis, P.C. Moraldo, and P.C. Bisram.

All these officers alleged that they arrested two Venezuelans, Louis Britto and Henry Ramos, in Chacachacare with six and a half kilos of cocaine.

They further said that at about 7:00 pm that night, they all left La Tinta beach in two boats headed for Chaguaramas.

In the hired boat driven by Lincoln Charles were: Cpl. Sealey,

Cpl. Treia, P.C. Abraham, P.C. Moraldo, P.C. Fournellier, P.C. Bisram, P.C. Delfish, P.C. Austin and P.C. Narcis, and the two Venezuelans, Britto and Ramos.

In the boat seized from the Venezuelans were: Sgt. Sebro, Cpl. Bernard, P.C. Black, P.C. Craig, P.C. Campo, P.C. Kennedy, and P.C. Salvary. The money and the cocaine, we are told, was in the possession of Sgt. Sebro at this time.

On their way back, they say, the seas became rough and turbulent. Somewhere in the vicinity of 'Chac' the hired boat had rapidly gone under. Sebro, Bernard, Campo and Kennedy remained holding on to the boat, but Black and Craig swam to shore. Salvary perished. The 21 kilos of cocaine and $10,000.00 US were lost. The other boat made it to Staubles Bay, where they deposited Britto and Ramos and made their way back to Chaguaramas in a coast guard vessel, where they rescued their colleagues.

Britto and Ramos were charged for trafficking narcotics, and it took more than two years for their case to come on for hearing at the Assizes in Port of Spain. My dear friend and colleague Carlyle Walters and I were retained to represent Britto and Ramos, and we had the benefit of a translator, my dear friend and colleague, Ms. Jackie Anderson. Jackie spoke fluent Spanish and assisted me whenever a case involved Venezuelan nationals. I shall always be grateful to her. Representing the D.P.P. was my learned friend Ms. Paula May Weekes, who is today our esteemed President of the Republic of Trinidad and Tobago.

The case started before Mr. Justice Lennox Deyalsingh in the P.O.S. Assizes and on the 18th of July 1989 the learned judge directed the jury to return a verdict of not guilty. The Judge actually said before freeing the two men that the case gave him "a very uneasy feeling and left many unanswered questions."

This came about because the police witnesses were caught lying all the way through the case for the prosecution. It was rather embarrassing really, but it was surreal.

Suspicion was rampant. The Judge was skeptical, the jury was perplexed. The press presented the whole of the story as they knew it to be, and the people of Trinidad and Tobago became restless and suspicious. As a result, on Friday the 28th of July 1989, a mere ten days after Britto and Ramos were freed, the Acting President and Commander in Chief of the Republic of Trinidad and Tobago, Mr. Michael Williams, ordered a Commission of Inquiry to be held into the circumstances of the disappearance and/or death of P.C. Salvary, and of all activities by members of the police service which led to the arrest of Britto and Ramos.

Three very good men were appointed by the President to be the commissioners, Mr. Frank Solomon, Dr. Peter Lewis and Lt. Commander Laurence Goldstraw. This commission was ordered to do its work and report thereon "with the utmost dispatch."

Accordingly, the Commission of Inquiry began sitting on Monday 7th of August 1989.

Sixty-six witnesses gave evidence at the Inquiry. The police witnesses gave their version of what happened. I sat through it all because I represented Mrs. Salvary, the mother of the dead police officer. But it was really pathetic to hear those narcotic squad men give their evidence. It was almost as if they lined up before a teacher who made sure they all were saying the same thing. But then many of them forgot what it was they had to say, so now, it became real 'ole mas'.

The Commission of Inquiry ended on 20th December 1989.

It is now known that the Commission of Inquiry, in its report to His Excellency, recommended that the report be forwarded to the Director of Public Prosecutions to determine whether several police officers should be criminally charged. It seems that because of this mandate, the entire Report of the Commissioners into the La Tinta incident was kept away from the public. It couldn't be released because it would be prejudicial to their cases.

Let me explain what that meant. Between the sixteen officers who were involved and gave evidence at the Commission of Inquiry, they had themselves charged hundreds of citizens for various offences before the La Tinta Inquiry. And those matters were already before the courts. So, if the State were to charge them with committing crimes in La Tinta, all their cases would be dismissed. And also, the State would most likely be sued by many of the defendants whose cases were dismissed.

Imagine that! So it meant that the country was deprived of the truth because these police officers were likely to face criminal charges. Some of the charges contemplated were conspiracy to pervert the course of public justice, perjury and trafficking in narcotics. What a mess. But Hold. Consider what happened next...

On the 15th of March 1991, sixteen of the La Tinta policemen were suspended, but lo and behold, on the 25th of June 1992, ten of the sixteen had their suspensions lifted by the Police Service Commission. They were reinstated in the Police Service of Trinidad and Tobago and assigned to duty in Police Stations all across the country.

And on Wednesday the 7th of February 1996, the three officers accused of conspiracy to pervert the course of justice and perjury were freed after the State offered no further evidence.

By this time, governments had changed, and so what was good for one government was not good for the other. But the people of Trinidad and Tobago were entitled to know what the commissioners found. They were never ever told.

The Commissioners reported to our President that they had concluded their Inquiry and that they had come to the following Conclusion:

<u>48.1</u> Whatever may have been the system of values, if any, which regulated or in any significant way affected the behavior and attitudes of Sgt. Sebro and the men under his command at the La Tinta operation (and be it noted, that almost the entire Narcotics Squad was involved), respect for the truth or for the rule of law found no place in it.

<u>48.2</u> Professionalism, in the normal acceptation of the term, was not a characteristic of the Squad. Their concept of professionalism amounted, at best, to no more than a boastful awareness of their own importance to a society they understood to be helpless without them to defend itself against the threat of destruction by drugs. The outstanding feature of those members of the squad who appeared before us, was the casual and utter cynicism with which they addressed the problems created for them by the Commission of Inquiry.

There was no member of the Squad who did not lie to the Commission and there was none who had the least compunction about doing so.

Their attitudes ranged from immature and even puerile defiance, as in the case of P.C. Delfish, to the pious disingenuousness of Cpl. Sealey, to the outrageous mendacity of Treia, and the sinister and unnerving instability of Kennedy, and finally, to the arrogant and bombastic prevarications of Sebro himself.

<u>48.3</u> They all, in their separate ways, lied to us. The style and quality of their dishonesties would vary, not unnaturally perhaps, from personality to personality, as each presented

ritually his prepared litany. Some may have seemed more offensive than others, perhaps because they gave the impression of enjoying themselves too much, like Kennedy, or because, like Bisram, their lies were crude and delivered without flair or sophistication. **But in the final analysis they impressed us as being a thoroughly dishonest lot, who down to a man, had no conception that to lie to a public inquiry was in any way unprofessional or morally reprehensible. They gave the impression rather, that they felt it was their duty to do so, and that to support the common invention was an honorable thing to do, rather than the opposite. It was not that they lacked morality. It was that their morality was corrupt. They had ceased to be accountable to the law or to their profession, their community, or their country. They were accountable only to one another.**

They presented to us a cynical corps of outlaws, dangerously vested with the special powers of policemen. Moreover, they enjoyed the privileges attendant upon being the elite of the police service, while being in reality, perfidious trustees of the public safety.

<u>48.4</u> **We examined them as thoroughly as we knew how and extended to them every opportunity to tell the truth. We used every inducement and threat that was psychologically or legally available to us to persuade them individually to break ranks and revert to honesty, but none, we regret to say, was even tempted.**

Those conclusions and the recommendations of the Commission of Inquiry were most probably thrown into a dustbin. But consider how greatly important that Inquiry Report was for the Nation. And to this day, the public has no idea what it said.

A few years ago, after the La Tinta episode, I had an occasion to go into the Santa Cruz Police Station and the officer in charge was Sebro, who was by that time an Inspector. He came from his office with a big smile and said loudly so all his subordinates could hear: "De Lima, is you? What can I do for you. Tell me?" I said I was sorry because I had the wrong Police Station and left. Imagine that! I wasn't afraid, you know. I was sad and indignant and 'damn vexed' too.

CHAPTER 16

THE LEGAL PROFESSION IN REAL TROUBLE

As I explained earlier, persons charged with serious crimes never reveal to their attorneys that they are guilty. However, I suspect that all that has changed now because some of the lawyers nowadays are criminals themselves, and they would break every rule and/or law to win a case.

I first saw this in the seventies, and being naïve, I didn't believe what I was seeing, but as time went by, I encountered it over and over. Jury tampering and interfering with witnesses and in a few cases even murdering the witness. We had descended to a bad place. Truthfully, I was apprehensive to do any case in which there were multiple accused persons, because I was afraid of being compromised by some of the attorneys appearing for the co-accused.

And I have on several occasions refused a brief because of an attorney/attorneys who I learnt would be appearing for co-defendants in the case.

In the old days, one couldn't become a barrister-at-law unless one was able to obtain at least three testimonials from persons of repute, vouching for the integrity and respectability of the applicant. In those days, some people would laugh at that and others would even deem it discriminatory, etc. But, I promise you, there was a 'damn good reason' the colonial masters had that rule, and I would experience it fully in due course.

I must say though, that bad behavior at the Bar only came about because the younger attorneys saw what was done by a few of their seniors, and thought it was o.k. to emulate them.

I remember well doing a murder Preliminary Inquiry in a country court in a case that involved multiple accused and lawyers. When the main witness for the State took the witness stand, he announced that he really knew nothing about the case, but that the police had forced him to sign his witness statement. Everybody in the court was shocked. Then one of the lawyers at the Bar table began laughing, and he said to his colleagues that he had arranged for the witness to say what he said. The accused men were discharged. And I left that court a totally changed man. What is more, that lawyer rose to become 'Eminent Senior Counsel'.

CHAPTER 17

MURDER IN GRENADA – 'ISLAND IN THE SUN'

Probably the most beautiful Island in the Caribbean, Grenada lies about 110 miles north of Trinidad. It is called 'Spice Island' because of the nutmeg and various other spices that are grown there, some of which you can actually smell as you drive around the Island.

The beaches are among the finest in the world, and most importantly, the Grenadian people are lovely and kind and plentifully honest.

What is more, this little island has produced so many good and wonderful Caribbean persons, such as Jennifer Hosten, the Mighty Sparrow, Buzz Uriah Butler, Kirani James, Baron David Pitt, Lt. Julian Marryshow, Dr. Peter Gentle, and many more. I have always felt that Grenada was part of Trinidad and Tobago, because I grew up knowing so many Grenadian people, and I remember, as a little boy, hearing that when the police in Trinidad would come to arrest the Grenadian illegal immigrants to send them back to Grenada, the test they would employ was to ask them to say the following words: "BOX, ORANGE, GOD and DOG", to which they would answer: "BAAX, AARINGE, GAAD and DAAG". But they are a lovely people.

THE MURDER CASE

Sometime in late 1970, I was retained by a Ms. Catherine Lazarus to go to Grenada to defend her brother Errol Jeremiah at the Assizes. He was charged for murdering one Herbert Jansen, aged 42, who was the son of the Dutch Ambassador to Grenada.

I arrived in Grenada four days before the trial started and went directly to Her Majesty's Prison, in Richmond Hill, St. George's to take instructions from my client. Thereafter, a man called Hugo Blanco befriended me and insisted that he would take me around the Island. He did that and filled me in with all the gossip he thought I should know about the case.

Errol Jeremiah was a young Trinidadian, aged twenty at the time, and he was staying with his sister and her common law husband, an Englishman called Knight, and their two-year-old daughter at their home on Grand Anse beach. His defence was that he was strolling along the beach at about 5:30 pm with the two-year-old girl in his arms when Jansen, who appeared to be drunk, attacked him with a knife. He dropped the child and defended himself, during the course of which he was able to take away the knife from Jansen, and in the course of defending himself, he stabbed Jansen, who died ten days after in the Grenada General hospital.

Instructions simple as Simon. No witnesses, other than the two-year-old, who couldn't give evidence anyway. Jansen went into the Grenada Hospital and the next day the police arrived and took statements. Errol gave them a statement, and so did Catherine and her husband Knight. It appears that Jansen was a difficult and worthless man and decided he would not give a statement to the police.

Anyway, after remaining in the Hospital for ten days, Jansen took a turn for the worse and died. It shocked everyone, including his attending surgeon, Dr. Friday, who was an eminent man and was of the opinion that there was no reason he should die. The surgery was quite minor and was successful, and so the death was a mystery.

So everybody thought, until it was discovered that Jansen, who was an alcoholic, had his girlfriend, a Ms. Sinannan from Trinidad, bringing Alcolada Glacial, an alcohol-based hair tonic, into the hospital for him every day. He drank the hair tonic, causing the wound to perforate.

I stayed at the St. James Hotel, which was within walking distance from the court, and I would walk to and from court every day.

Staying at the hotel when I was there was a very gentle, elderly man named Edwin Heyliger. He was a Queens Counsel and had practiced throughout the Caribbean for many years, and was by then gearing down to retirement. I was so fortunate and grateful to make his acquaintance, and we would talk every night for a few hours about my case and about his life and experiences at the Bar. I shall always remember him, because he guided me like a father up to the end of my case there.

Anyway, the case was called before His Lordship, Mr. Justice St. Louis, and it lasted three days, after which the jury returned a verdict of guilty of manslaughter.

We were able to adduce evidence about his girlfriend taking the hair tonic into the hospital for him. After hearing what I had to say by way of mitigation, the judge passed a sentence of four years hard labor on Errol Jeremiah, which I thought was very lenient.

Before leaving the court, I went to the prisoners' holding bay to say goodbye to Jeremiah. I told him that I was quite pleased with the verdict, though I really hoped the jury would have returned a verdict of not guilty on the grounds of self defence.

Then he virtually floored me by what he said. He was elated about the verdict and said: "Boss, thank you so much. You saved my life. I did not know anything about this murder. On the evening it took place, there was a fight between my brother-in-law Knight and Jansen, and it was my brother-in-law who stabbed him. I was not even there. But Knight offered to pay me $100,000.00 if I would say it was me. Both he and my sister explained that they had the Hotel on Grand Anse Beach and they would lose everything if Knight was charged. And that the fight was because Jansen was having an affair with Catherine who wished to end it."

I was stunned and I asked, "But, they hang people here. What would have happened if you had lost the case?" "Nah!" he said. "They tell me they would pay good money and bring a good lawyer from Trinidad. Not to worry. And what is more, they placed the $100,000.00 in my Bank account in Trinidad right away."

Then I left the Court and walked towards my Hotel. On my way, a black chauffeur driven car pulled up alongside me and the person sitting in the back seat wound down the glass. It was Prime Minister Eric Gairy. He shook my hand and said, "Mr. De Lima, I would like to invite you to a cocktail party I'm having this evening." I thanked him but explained that I was booked on a flight to Trinidad, so could not accept his invitation.

I left Grenada a few hours later. I think of Grenada every time I hear Belafonte singing 'Island in the Sun'.

CHAPTER 18

NOT EASY TO HANG A CHINAMAN

The Chinese came to Trinidad a long time ago. In fact, they were here even before the (East) Indians arrived. The first group of Chinese arrived in Trinidad in 1806, aboard a ship called 'The Fortitude', whereas the first Indians arrived aboard the 'Fatel Rozack' in 1845.

Both came as indentured laborers to work in the sugar and cacao estates, and when they arrived, apart from the colonial masters, they met the Africans who were here since 1639, and who were made to suffer and endure slavery.

The Chinese in Trinidad have not only been industrious, but have excelled in many disciplines. They have been exemplary citizens, and a Chinaman, Sir Solomon Hochoy, was the first Governor General of Trinidad and Tobago from 1962 until 1972.

THE CASE

Sometime in the early 1970s, there was a parlor/rum shop in Park Street, Port of Spain, directly opposite the Globe cinema. It was owned and operated by a Chinese family called Ping that had not too long before come from China. Ping lived at the back of the shop together with his attractive wife, Mylin, and his brother Soong.

A very well-known police Inspector used to visit Ping's shop in the evenings as a customer, and after a while he began making advances to Mylin, who was very young and impressionable.

One day Soong caught the Inspector kissing and caressing Mylin whilst Ping was out on business. Incensed by this, after the Inspector left, Soong took a Chinese chopper (hatchet) and hacked her to death. As a result, he was charged for her murder.

The case was tried in the Port of Spain Assizes and Soong was convicted and sentenced to death. Accordingly, he was taken to the condemned cell in Port of Spain to await his execution.

Shortly after his conviction, I was approached by a Chinese shopkeeper in Toco who asked me if I would represent Soong in his appeal. I agreed, and he said he would contact me in a week or so to arrange payment of my fee, etc. But before he was able to do that, Soong killed himself in the condemned cell. It was in the papers that he had committed suicide in his cell. He did so by tying his bed sheet around his neck and bobbing his head up and down under his bed until he severed his spinal chord and died. This took place in the early hours of the morning.

When I next saw the Toco shopkeeper, he told me this in his inimitable Chinese way, "Mr. De Lima, this is what happen: Chinese Hierarchy gave consideration to Soong case. They meet and make decision. They listen all evidence. They say Soong wrong to kill Mylin because she not his wife. They say that if Ping had kill her, they would support him full, but not Soong."

He continued, "So Chinese Hierarchy send messenger to Soong to inform him their decision. And that is why you no hear from me no more."

When I visited the Prison sometime later, one of the officers told me that the day before Soong killed himself, two elderly Chinamen visited him for about fifteen minutes and that they spoke to him only in Chinese. Then they got up, bowed to him, and left.

I was very interested to know what these two Chinamen had said to Soong, and eventually my Toco friend told me. He said they told him that they were sent by the Chinese Hierachy to inform him that they had concurred that what he did was wrong, and that they would not support him financially or in any other way. And that for the past 164 years ever since the Chinese were in Trinidad, no Chinaman had ever been hanged. So that in the circumstances, it would be good of him to ensure that he was not the first to suffer that fate and bring shame and scandal to the Chinese community.

CHAPTER 19

CLARITA THE 'PARANG' QUEEN

What is Parang? It is folk music of Trinidad and Venezuela, showing how close we have been and still are.

Clarita Rivas was named the First Parang Queen of Trinidad in 1974, and she and her brothers Alfredo, Aristo and William played every Christmas season with the band known as Sharp Los Pavitos.

Clarita is a lovely person. She is not only talented as a musician, playing the guitar and the quatro and maracas, but she sings beautifully. More than all of that, she loves people. Like the De Lima's, the Rivas family is essentially Venezuelan, and are what we call in Trinidad "Cacao Spanish". Our two families have been friends for more than sixty years.

Clarita, who is a spinster, and two of her brothers, Aristo and Alfredo, lived on a property in Buena Vista Road in St. Joseph. They have lived there for more than fifty years and are known as peace loving people to all the neighbors and people living in Maracas Valley. Her brothers lived there with their wives and children, and all was good, until the evening of Monday 2nd of March 1998, when all hell broke loose.

At about 9.00 pm that night, a car pulled up in front our home in Santa Margarita Circular Road, St. Augustine, and Alfredo and Clarita were sitting in the back seat. A friend of theirs was driving the car and he explained to me that Clarita had just a few minutes before shot Aristo, and it appears that he died. She was obviously in shock, and I immediately got a drink of brandy and gave it to her.

She related to me that she had been unwell for the past week, and was under doctor's care as she was told that she was on the verge on having a nervous breakdown. As a result, she was bedridden for more than five days. Earlier that evening, Aristo, who lived in the rooms next to her with his children, permitted his son to play the radio very loudly, to the extent she was unable to rest, far less sleep. She complained to him at least three times that evening, but the noise continued until she could not stand it anymore. Whereupon she took up a revolver which her deceased father had left in the house, and she went to Aristo's room to complain yet again. But when he saw her, he began arguing with her, and she fired the gun until there were no bullets left. She swore that she had no recollection of actually firing the gun.

This is one of the saddest cases I ever had to do.

I accompanied her to the St. Joseph Police Station shortly after, and she gave the police a full statement recounting everything that happened. Understandably, she was detained by the police, and two days later she was charged with murdering Aristo.

The case took about eighteen months to reach the Assizes, and when it got there, the Judge assigned to do it was Mr. Justice Stanley John. We made it clear to the Prosecution that we wished to plead guilty to the lesser count of manslaughter and the DPP, Mr. Clebert Brooks, very kindly agreed to accept the plea.

Accordingly, Clarita pleaded guilty to manslaughter, and was asked if she had anything to offer as to her sentence. Through me, she explained what had happened and that she was devastated because of what she had done and was contrite. We presented several character witnesses' statements to the court on her behalf, and of course, the most important and moving of all was when Aristo's wife and children pleaded for leniency for her. Many persons in the court were in tears. The Judge adjourned for a few days to consider what sentence would be appropriate.

When the case resumed on the 10th of August 1999, the learned Judge spoke to Clarita in open court. Among the things he said was that he understood her remorse and contrition, and that what she had suffered and continued to suffer was far more than any custodial sentence he could impose. He told her to go home and keep the peace for three years. Clarita left the court and went directly to Aristo's grave to ask his forgiveness, and she gave thanks to Almighty God.

Clarita is still the best maracas player in Trinidad. If you don't believe me, just google: <Clarita Rivas>.

Parang Queen – Clarita Rivas

CHAPTER 20

HORSERACING, BOXING AND FISHING

I loved each of these sports, equally. And I devoted time to each of them, equally.

HORSERACING

Ever since I was a little boy growing up in Cascade, I loved horseracing. I remember, at age ten (which means 1950), going to the Savannah early in the morning – during school vacation of course – to see the horses gallop in preparation for the upcoming race meeting. I had my notebook with me, my father's binoculars, and later, I was given a stop watch as a Christmas present.

In those days, there were three race tracks, Port of Spain Savannah, Santa Rosa in Arima, and Union Park in San Fernando. Each of these tracks were operated by a club, i.e., the Trinidad Turf Club, the Arima Race Club and the Union Park Race Club. But the overmaster of them all was the Trinidad Turf Club, which introduced the sport to Trinidad sometime around 1857.

I loved horses and I loved to see them race. And I enjoyed giving people tips about the horses I saw galloping in the wee hours of the morning in the Savannah. I remember a particular trainer who would gallop his charges just shortly before the sun came up, so that onlookers would not see how well his horses were training.

My parents were friendly with the Winfield Scott family, who had a stud farm in Diego Martin, where we children were allowed to ride an old, retired, docile mare named 'La Platta'. It was great fun.

On race days, I would be invited by the Scotts to go with them. Pierrepoint, who was my age, was my friend, and we were experts at forcasting how the races would run. It really was a wonderful time. I remember meeting Chally Jones[4] at the Scott's home sometime around 1952. Dr. Steve Bennett brought him to a dinner party there and I remember him wearing a cork hat. He was only twelve years old and he was already riding horses. We have remained friends since that time, and his son Douglas is very friendly with my son Damon. They are both commercial airline pilots in the U.S.A.

Mr. Winfield Scott was an ardent racing man, and he is among the people who did so very much for racing in Trinidad and Tobago. He brought to Trinidad some of the finest racehorses, including Muskatoon, Bounty, Westend, Ostara, Glint-of-Sun and so many more.

Among the great horses I was privileged to see race at our Savannah were Airofaith, Darjeeling, Ligan, Jetsam, Baby Bird, Flagship, Royal Visit, Sugar Lady, and the fantastic Mentone. And these came after many greats which were before my time, such as Take-a-Light, War Lord, Ras Taffare, Gleneagle, and Ocean Pearl. I often tell people about Baby Bird, which was the smallest racehorse I ever saw. She was as small as a donkey, but

---

4. Chally Jones was a well-known and successful jockey from Barbados

did she have speed! She was a creole bred by Mr. Lionel Gittens, one of my father's great friends, and known to me as 'Uncle Lio.' Baby Bird beat all the other horses in the sprints so that she was promoted to 'A' Class, where she had to compete with the imported thoroughbreds – which she did with distinction. She beat the 'A' Class as well before she was retired.

There are always debates and arguments as well as to which of all the horses was the best to race in Trinidad. My dear friend, Dr. Steve Bennett, always said that in his opinion the Jamaican grey creole 'Bruceontheloose' and 'Mentone' were the two best horses to race in Trinidad and maybe he was right. He knew horses inside out. It was certainly a real privilege for me to have known not only this great man, but his father Mr. Penn Bennett, who himself was an icon of horse racing, having, like Steve, been both an outstanding jockey and a trainer in his time.

Trinidad always had owners who have stood up for the sport. People like the Latours, the Scotts, the Barnards, the Bennetts, the Poon Tips, the Samlalsinghs (Old Man Sam, to Merlin and Mike), the Gittens, the Gilettes, the Samaroos, the Trestrails, the Maharajs, the Lourencos, the O'Briens, the Leotauds, and Kama Maharaj.

And there were very good trainers as well. They were all decent people who simply loved the sport for what it was. People like Eric 'Colt' Durant, Joe Hadeed, Edmund De Freitas (himself an outstanding jockey), his brother Patrick De Freitas (my trainer), Mano 'Killer' Joseph, Ian "Fat Man" Gordon, Hollis and Henry Bhopa, Curtis Aird, John O'Brien, John Leotaud, Elton Harper, Boboy Maharaj, Glen Mendez, Pepsi Gobin and so many more.

Partnership is 'Leakiship'

Sometime in a December of the early 60's, my father was sitting at his desk in the Trinidad Jewellery when Mr. Matthew Gonsalves, also known as 'Mr. Elite', a very good friend of his, walked in and sat down opposite my dad.[5] He explained to Dad that he had a problem, and it was this: He was a half-owner with Mr. M.E.R. Bourne of a horse called Flagship that Bourne had brought down from England. The horse was a good horse and had won a couple of times. He said the problem was that he and Mr. Bourne couldn't get along for many reasons, and so he wanted out of this partnership arrangement. Dad advised him to approach Bourne and suggest that they appoint a valuator, acceptable to them both, and have him put a value on the horse. That having been done, he suggested that one of them buy out the other. Mr. Gonsalves did exactly as Dad suggested and Mr. Bourne bought him out.

Two weeks later, on Boxing Day, Flagship duly won his race, but as he was returning to the Winners Enclosure, he dropped dead of heart failure.

The Decline of Horse Racing in Trinidad

It really is a shame to see what racing has come to in Trinidad and Tobago. It's a disgrace and I am told that it is on its last legs.

I must say this. I never agreed with removing racing from the Savannah. I could never understand why that was done, other than an explanation that Dr. Williams, the Prime Minister, did not like racing and decided that it should be held away from the Savannah. I so remember well, that on a race day the people from the surrounding areas like Laventille, Belmont, Cascade/ St Anns, Maraval and St. James would be seen on the roads hurrying up to make sure they got to the Savannah before the first race, which was usually about 12:30 pm.

And the people on the inner field known as 'grounds' had their games, and 'hoopla', a game where one tries to throw a hoop over an object to win it. There was 'Over and Under the Lucky 7', 'Spot the Ball', 'Hit the Ball Head Man', where you would

---

5. Matthew Gonsalves owned the Elite shirt factory in Trinidad.

throw a tennis ball at the bald head of a man who placed his head through a hole in a canvass about twenty feet away. And there was 'Brand Dip'. Those games were all great fun.

Race day on the grounds was considered a family outing. It really was so lovely. And you could place your horse bets on the grounds as well. Even little children loved to go to races with their parents, to both see the horses and have great fun on the grounds of the Savannah.

Jennifer and I owned about eight horses over the years, and we were quite successful. Among them were DARK MOON, SORAYA, GOING GOING GONE, FUNNY MUNNY, and ADIOS AMIGOS. SORAYA had the distinction of winning the first Breeders Cup Fillies Race in Trinidad and Tobago. We were very proud of all our horses, regardless of their track performances, because we loved each one of them for the joy they gave to us over the years.

People have their views about the Racing Industry in Trinidad and Tobago, and I respect all of them but I also have my opinion, which is that the minute Government entered into the realm of horseracing, the whole thing went awry. I am now old enough to give proper reflection and interpretation to many things I experienced.

I was involved as counsel in the Noble Mark case against the Trinidad Turf Club in 1975. In my opinion The Club was wrong to reject the entry of Noble Mark for their Christmas Meeting. They did so on spurious grounds, and Noble Mark's owner Merlin Samlalsingh applied to the High Court for Judicial Review and he was successful. The Club was faced with a situation, either accept the horse's entry or there would be no racing on Boxing Day. The Club relented. But that, I fear, was the death knell of racing at the Savannah. It spurred the coming of the Trinidad and Tobago Racing Authority, and the almost immediate removal of racing from the Savannah. Merlin had succeeded but consider what was to come.

'The Hand Brakes Stakes'

This is not to say that racing didn't have its crooks as well. On Saturday 15th of July 1978, there was a most scandalous incident in racing in Trinidad and Tobago.

During the course of the Port of Spain TTC Mid-Summer meeting, nine jockeys got together and decided to fix a race so that they and their friends would make a killing. They held a meeting at the home of one of the jockeys in Woodbrook two nights before race day. The meeting took place around 8:00 pm, and the nine jockeys sat around a table which was laid out, with pen, paper, a glass of water and a race program before each one of them – just like any Board of Directors meeting.

Then the lead jockey, who was a known crook, called the meeting to order. He explained briefly what the meeting was about and said that it was decided that the 7th Race was the one that was selected because there were only nine horses entered and it was controllable. It was agreed by them all that a particular horse would be allowed to win, and that they would all restrain their mounts to ensure that. In other words, the race was fixed.

However, on race day everything went awry. The race started and the horse the jockeys wanted to win was beaten by the favorite. All hell broke loose in the jockeys room, and the stewards became suspicious and summoned an inquiry. Half of them were banned for six months, and the leader for one year. He was a brilliant jockey, and it was inconceivable that he would stoop to dishonesty. But life plays out. A few years after this incident, he fell from a horse at the said Savannah and severed his spinal chord, and was unable to walk for the rest of his life.

Challenor (Chally) Lynch Jones, who I have known since we were both twelve, has always had a good sense of humor. In 1972, he was awarded the MBE by Her Majesty the Queen for being an outstanding jockey in the Caribbean.

When he was summoned to meet with the Governor in Barbados, Chally asked him if this award was going to cost him anything. The Governor replied, "No, no, Chally, this doesn't cost. It's free." Chally then said, "Well Sir, in that case I think I would like to have two!"

I know that my view will not be in accord with those of many racing people, but I'll give it anyway. I am of the opinion that racing began to die the day it left the Savannah, the 'Big Yard', for Arima. It lost the crowds in no time, because the ready-made fans who lived nearby found it difficult, and/or inconvenient, or frankly impossible, to travel by taxi to Arima every Saturday. That, together with the influx of so many bookmaking shops all over the country ensured the slow but positive demise of the sport.

The bookmakers became leaches, they sucked the industry dry. Every so often they would ostensibly donate a prize for racing at the Arima track, but the sport was long already moribund, and they knew that. But they didn't care, as long as they made their money by attracting the crowds that couldn't go to Arima and enticing away those who could. I often wonder whether they had an impact in the decision to stop racing in the Savannah. But, say what! We'll never know.

I detested going to races in Arima. It was impersonal and very dull. One got the impression that the races were being run there for one purpose only, that was to gamble and make money. It really had nothing to do with the horses, their breeding and their form, etc. It really was, and still is, solely about money.

Gone forever was the family aspect of racing, and the youths began avoiding the track. The die was cast. Then, like many of my dear racing friends, I too stopped going to races. The whole industry just began to fold up before our eyes. Spurious individuals began owning racehorses, and this was allowed because so many of the genuine racehorse lovers simply packed up and stopped racing entirely.

Before leaving this topic, I must make mention of the very many good, honest and respectable people I met in racing who became my friends. They are so many that I can't remember them all, so please forgive me if I omit to mention any of them. They include Joe Hadeed, Ray Diffenthaler, Dr. Steve Bennett, Mr. Penn Bennett (Icons of T&T racing), Merlin Samlalsingh, Ray Barnard, Ernie Melville, Frank Latour, Aldwyn Poon Tip, Colt Durant, Mano Joseph, Henry Bhopa, Juan Mosca, Elton Harper, Dr. Johnny Wharton, Gordon and Dorothy Trestrail, the sisters Chay and Soo Poy (gentlewomen par excellence), Michael 'Joey' Carew, Rolf Bartholo, Kama Maharaj, Ronald Mathieu and many more. I salute them all.

I love betting on grey horses. I think this goes back to the late forties when I accompanied my uncle to a Santa Rosa race day in Arima. In one of the races there was a grey horse called 'Distinction' and I insisted that my uncle should bet on him. He duly won, and paid $25.00 to win. My uncle was very pleased and gave me twenty dollars. I never forgot that.

BOXING

Many people consider boxing a cruel sport. I loved boxing and from the age of nine, I myself boxed.

In the late 1940's, St.Mary's College put on a Boxing night every year in which there was a program of usually twelve boxing matches, commencing with the Juniors who were about 9, 10 and 11 years old, then onto the Mid-Students (12, 13, and 14) , and ending the evening with the Seniors (15, 16).

It was a grand event. The ring was constructed in the middle of the school courtyard and there were lights and the whole works. The event usually started at 7:00 pm on a Friday evening and the last bout would begin around 10 pm. It was like a miniature Madison Square Garden, and each annual event would be attended by the parents and friends of the students. The crowd was usually about five hundred people.

There was a professional referee, Mr. Louis Baradas, in attendance, together with three judges selected from C.L Williams, Juan Reece, Fitz Oliver Thompson and Edgar Gaston Johnson. The contestants were attired in white shorts, white merino[6] and white socks and tennis shoes and one would wear a red sash and the other a blue sash.

Among the good boxers of my day at the college were: Everard Gordon, Carl Berridge, Dennis and Ken Ecalante, Garnet Rowley, Andy Graeham, Reds Graeham, Jeffrey "Chipsy" Mahon, Neil Xavier, Roy Cazabon, Selwyn Haywood, Vin Quesnel, Hugh Moze and Anthony Nieves.

I was privileged to box for three years at St. Mary's – 1949, 1950 and 1951 – and I won only once. In those days, boxing was a very popular sport. The great Joe Louis was the heavyweight champion of the world, and fabulous boxers like Rocky Marciano, Jersey Joe Walcott, Archie Moore, Sugar Ray Robinson and Ezzard Charles were around.

There was no television then, and when there was a world championship fight, everybody in Trinidad would huddle around the radio, in those days called 'Reddifusion', to listen. Those fights usually took place late at night, so children had to have the permission of their parents to stay up. That was easy to get because the parents would stay up as well.

I must say that boxing taught me discipline from an early age. I knew, even from that time, that if you boxed you should never take unfair advantage of another in a fist fight or at all. That indeed, it is your business to ensure that you learn to control your temper in life. And also, and most importantly, that you never hit a man when he's down. And that means 'down' in any way. Also, that means you always abide by the Judge's decision.

The sport of Boxing is no longer what it was. With the passing

---

6. slang for a T-shirt

of Mohammed Ali, whom I believe was the greatest boxer of all time, boxing is in decline. Today, I don't know who the heavyweight champ of the world is. And I really don't want to know, because I have now lost all interest in boxing. When Mohammed Ali left, that was it for me, because I consider him the best, and I had seen the best. May he Rest in Peace.

Over the years, Trinidad produced some good boxers. There was Gentle Daniel, Yaq Subero, Yolande Pompey, Claud Noel and Leslie Stewart.

They were all international stars. Trinis again.

FISHING

This is a hobby I loved so very much. I became a fisherman at age six. At that age, I was down the Islands on Monos with my parents, when I first threw out a fishing line from the jetty and caught a fish. It was a small fish, but it was a fish. I had caught my first fish. I never forgot that.

In those days, my parents leased an island home called 'Paradise Bay' on Monos Island, now owned by my dear friend Robert Johnson, and we would go 'down the Islands' most weekends. I made friends with the fishermen there and every so often they would take me with them when they were going to fish. It was 1947/8 and in those days there were no fast boats. In fact, the boat, which my two fisherman friends Andre Medina and Lionel Pegus had, was a small, open pirogue called 'ANNA' (named after their employer Ms. Anna Siegert), which had a two-horsepower engine. It therefore could only travel at about three miles an hour, and the engine made such a constant noise it could be heard a mile away. That engine we called a 'Putt Putt' because that is how it sounded: 'Putt, putt, putt, putt...', and so on.

But I learned to fish with my two friends Andre and Lio. First they taught me to bank, i.e., to drop a line with bait from a stationary boat that was anchored. Then they showed me the art of trolling where a baited line is drawn through the water, and finally, when I was big enough to accompany them, they introduced me to Pag (Cubera snapper) fishing. We would go in 'ANNA' to Chacachacare island, just under the lighthouse, in the night time, during the falling tide and anchor the boat about fifty yards from the cliff.

The Cubera is a nocturnal feeder and we worked it out over the years that the best time to catch them was during the falling tide in the new Moon. (Money can't pay for that tip!)

The Cubera is the largest snapper known, and can grow to as much as 350 pounds. We would catch them in the vicinity of 20 to 50 pounds and that was fun enough. Of course, in those days, as soon as we caught one good-sized one, we would break anchor and head home, because we wouldn't have ice on board, and we had to ensure the fish didn't go bad (rot) on us, and remembering we had at least ninety minutes to travel in the 'Putt Putt' to reach our bay.

I fished as a hobby all my life, and over the years I have owned several pirogue boats which I kept in Las Cuevas Bay, from where I would embark when I went fishing. I worked it out that the best fishing grounds were past Maracas Bay going east on the north coast, so the best place to keep the boat was Las Cuevas, which would be so much closer to the fishing banks. I kept my boats one at a time in Las Cuevas since 1968, and as a result I am known to, and am friendly with, most of the people of that area.

Cecil Mc Lean, known as 'Haraze', and Cornell Clement, also called 'Hoggie' have looked after my boats and me over the years, and I owe them a great debt of gratitude, because not only were they fishing colleagues, but they became family to me and my children over the years. Nothing was too much for them to do for me and my family. I remember well many times when I would be late in returning to the beach, one of them would come out or send one of their friends out to make sure I was safe. We had no cell phones then.

On the 11th of July 1981, a most important date, my brother-in-law Anthony Boos, who had bought himself a small pirogue, asked if I would take him to the Pag bank in Chacachacare. I agreed, and four of us, Anthony, my fishing partner Sankar Kalloo, his friend Bal and I, set out at about 5:00 pm in his new boat which he named 'Katja'.

We arrived on bank at about 6:30 pm and began fishing just as the tide started falling. At about 7:00 pm we landed a huge Cubera snapper which we discovered later weighed 87 pounds. We immediately broke anchor and headed for home. Anthony was so proud and kept saying that the luck was brought by his new boat. Maybe he was right. But I swear I never saw a bigger red fish.

I thought we had broken the record, only to discover that the statistics which were kept at the Trinidad Yacht Club revealed that our catch was only about 27th in rank. The biggest was caught in 1941 and weighed 218 pounds. It was caught by Arnim Tardieu from Chaguaramas.

I continued fishing as a hobby until about seven years ago (2015). I stopped because it was dangerous to fish at night, since the drug runners transport a lot of their supplies then.

The last time I fished at night was in August of 2015. Hoggie and I left Las Cuevas Bay in my pirogue 'Spanish Prayers' at about 6:00 pm and went to Paria Bay to fish Pag. We arrived there at about 8:00 pm and began fishing.

Fish were biting, so by 10:00 pm we had caught about ten red fish; about thirty pounds in all. Rain was falling, but we were sheltered because 'Spanish Prayers' had a hood.

At about 11:30 pm whilst we were fishing, Hoggie said to me: "Don't look back now, but there is a boat passing right behind us between us and the beach." I said nothing and when he told me it had left, I simply wound up my line and we left for home. I have never again been back in the sea at nighttime. As long ago as that I became aware that that was one of the ways that drugs and firearms were entering Trinidad.

Around the same time, a good friend of mine told me that he was accustomed to swimming in Macqueripe Bay, Chaguaramas, at about 6 am every morning for a few years, until one morning he saw a pirogue come ashore with about ten young Spanish-speaking women who were hurriedly taken away by a maxi taxi. Thereafter he stopped going to Macqueripe Bay.

I spoke to the Coast Guard about my experience, and I was told that my information would be noted and that they would get back to me. Of course, that never happened.

The people who own homes on Monos Island all know that a great amount of the transporting of drugs takes place right in front of their properties. Very often, they see the boats, travelling very fast at night, with no lights, but they are afraid to report it because on occasion Coast Guard vessels have been seen travelling in close proximity to some of the suspicious boats, whether in pursuit or in entourage, being uncertain.

Therefore, it must be that locking down the borders of Trinidad and Tobago is an absolute must if the authorities are serious about stopping Human and Narcotic trafficking. But for some unknown reason, there is not even any discussion about this. It seems taboo for the subject to be even raised.

The Drug and Human Trafficking Trade is destroying Trinidad and Tobago, and unless our Government realizes that and decides to deal harshly with it, all will be lost.

I have been in the Criminal Law Arena (Gayelle) for the past fifty-three years, and so I feel I am competent to suggest what I think would do the job.

I suggest:

1. Our Government invite the USA to partner with us in defeating this scourge.
2. Government introduces stringent border control. Use of drones important.
3. Stringent control over all vessels entering T&T. This includes yachts too.
4. Police Outposts at every Fishing depot, i.e., Las Cuevas, Carenage, La Filette, Moruga, etc., etc.
5. Thorough Inspection of all Containers entering and/or leaving Trinidad and Tobago.
6. Stringent control over who and what enters, and who and what leaves Piarco International and A.N.R. Robinson International Airports.

The BIG Fish

TRACK CONDITIONS : Firm   STARTER : Mr. Fred Harragin
RACE 1—AQUARIUS H'CAP — F 2 y.s. — 5 Furs. & 45 Yds. — $5,500; $2,438; $1,370;
$609.

NO.	HORSE	JOCKEY	WGT.		OWNER	DIVIDENDS	
1—FUNNY MUNNY		Regalado	117	Mr.	V. B. de Lima	$5.85	$1.65
2—Mr. BEE JAY (F)		Salandy	123	Mr.	M. Maharaj		$1.20
3—VICTORIA THE FIRST		Griffith	119	Mr.	K. Fook		$1.25
4—SHADOWFAX		Blades	113	Mr.	Crane	P'CAST :	$61.40

TIME : 1.03⅗   START : Good   FINISH : 1½, shorthead 3½, 1½
WINNER : br. c. Privy Vale/Dark Moon   TRAINED BY : M. Joseph

Jen and I lead in FUNNY MUNNY

CHAPTER 21

LOVE, CHERISH AND OBEY...(steups!)

One morning in 1969, I was sitting at my desk in Chambers in St.Vincent Street when the phone rang. It was Fr. Gerry Pantin, a Roman Catholic priest, and a good friend of mine. He explained that he had a parishioner who came to see him with a very strange problem. He was a young married man with a good job at one of the leading business houses in Trinidad, but that he was having serious financial problems because his wife was overspending all over the place and pledging his credit. As a result, he the husband, was going mad with worry and feared that at that rate, he would sooner or later be declared bankrupt. Fr. Pantin said that he had spoken to both the man and his wife, and he was unable to make head nor tail of what was happening. So he asked me if I would see them, and I agreed to.

The next day the husband came to see me and he explained how gravely worried he was about the situation and he wished he knew what to do. I asked a few questions. One was whether there was any problems in the marriage. He said there were none and that he and his wife had been happily married for five years, and they had two lovely children, a boy and a girl. I asked if she gambled or drank alcohol. Again, the answer was no. What is more, he assured me, she was a staunch catholic and attended mass regularly.

Like Fr. Gerry, I too was stumped. He appeared very genuine and likeable. But there had to be an answer so I asked him if I could talk with his wife. Of course, he said, and he set it up for her to come to see me the following day.

Next day she came with a year-old baby in her arms and sat across from me. I recounted what her husband had said to me and stressed how worried he was about her and the children and how much he said he loved them. She listened to me intently and sat silently for a few minutes. Then she asked, "Mr. De Lima, has my husband told you he has another woman?" I said he had not.

She said, "Well he has. And he has had her for more than a year. When I married him seven years ago, I had a very good job with a company as a stenographer. My salary was a good one. But my husband insisted that I should stop working when we married, and so I did. So, I obeyed and got a kick in my ass for obeying. I know it's only a matter of time before he walks out on me and I can't get a job now, my skill is rusty, and I would be lost with the two children.

So, I pledged his credit yes. I did so all around and I have sold some of the things I was able to sell. This is what I have. And I shall be able to survive with the children for a few months until I can work again."

She then took out a small Bank Deposit Book from her handbag and passed it to me. There was $78,000.00 in the account. I said I had no more questions and handed her back her bank book. She got up, thanked me for my time, said good-bye, and left with her baby.

About an hour after she left, her husband called on the telephone and asked if I had seen her. I told him I had, but that just like Fr. Pantin, I too was totally perplexed by the case and didn't have an idea what caused her to do what she did.

About two months after that, Jennifer and I were leaving for Miami on a BWIA flight at about 7:00 am. As we were taking our seats in the aircraft and I was placing my briefcase in the overhead compartment, a man bounced into me. I turned around to apologize and lo and behold, there was the husband, embarking with his companion, who was not his wife. He looked at me, apologized and sheepishly retreated to the back of the aircraft.

I never knew whether Fr. Pantin was also told the truth – and I never asked! There are some men who think that most women are stupid and are easily fooled especially where money transactions are concerned.

Many years ago, a T&T Government Minister approached a Lebanese business woman who was trying hard to sell a commercial property she owned on Duke Street in Port of Spain. He undertook to get for her one hundred thousand dollars more than she was asking, provided she agreed to pay him fifty thousand dollars by way of a commission. The woman agreed and the sale went through.

A few days after he paid her a visit in her office and reminded her about his commission, whereupon she promptly handed him a cheque, signed by her, for the sum of fifty thousand dollars. He smiled sheepishly, handed the cheque back to her, and walked away.

Woman so! Hats off to them.

CHAPTER 22

"NUFF IS ENOUGH...NAH TAKING MORE LICKS!"

Teresa Choon, 21 years old, was an attractive young Indian (East Indian) woman from the Biche area in Sangre Grande.

On Saturday the 1st of March 1969, the same day Inspector Cooke was murdered, Teresa was six months pregnant and was cooking dinner in her kitchen, awaiting the arrival of her husband, P.C. Anthony Choon, who had gone to a wedding in the district.

P.C. Choon and Teresa had been married for about five years and they had two children at the time. He was a policeman attached to a station in the area. Their marriage was, by and large, a good one, other than when he was unable to control himself whenever he drank. Then he would become nasty and violent. At these times he became aggressive and brutal, and would accuse Teresa of being unfaithful to him and all other sorts of things. He had a Jekyll and Hyde personality, and on occasion he actually beat her when in his drunken state. Of course, next day he would apologize. This went on for years.

At about 8:00 pm on that Saturday, he came home very drunk and attacked her while she was cooking in the kitchen. She pleaded over and over with him to behave himself, but he reacted by cuffing and slapping her and calling her a whore. He also laughed and boasted that he had earlier that evening taken a woman to the hospital to have his child. He struck her to the ground. Then he threw himself on the bed in their bedroom and began snoring.

By this time, Teresa was in a terrible state. She had been badly beaten up, and was thinking about the welfare of her unborn baby. She simply lost it, got up from the floor and walked into the kitchen where she boiled a full kettle of water, and took it into the bedroom and poured the water down the ear of her husband. She said that he jumped about five feet into the air and then fell back down. He died shortly after. She could take it no more.

Teresa was duly charged for murder, and a few days after the incident, I was retained by her mother to represent her.

One year later, the case came on for hearing at the Port of Spain Assizes before Mr. Justice Johnny Braithwaite. The State was represented by my dear and learned friend and sometimes fishing partner, Mr. Victor Nunez, who had a few days before indicated that the State intended to offer Teresa the opportunity of pleading guilty to the lesser count of manslaughter. She was pleased about this, and it was decided to accept the State's offer and plead guilty accordingly.

However, as we entered the court the first morning, I noticed a number of senior civil lawyers sitting at the Bar table. I enquired about this and I was informed that they were there with 'watching briefs' for a well-known Insurance Company as the deceased, P.C. Choon, was insured with their principal for a very large sum. Of course, if she pleaded guilty the Insurance Company would be relieved from having to pay anything because a crime would have been committed and the contract would be considered void.

I immediately went to speak with Teresa who was sitting in the Prisonerd's Dock and asked her if she was aware of all that I had been informed. She said she was not; whereupon I suggested to her that she ought to re-consider her decision to plead guilty to manslaughter, and with no hesitation she said: "In that case, Sir, I would like to plead not guilty!"

I immediately informed Mr. Nunez and we made a request to meet with the judge in his Chambers.

I remember how surprised the judge (Mr Justice Johnny Braithwaite) was, when I announced that my client wished to change her plea to not guilty. He said to me, "Mr. De Lima, I will tell you here and now, that it is my intention to release her on a bond right away if she pleads guilty!" I said to him that I appreciated what he had said, but I was not in a position at that time to tell him what it was that had made her change her mind.

I remember Mr. Brathwaite, in his inimitable Bajan accent, saying to me, "If you make us waste the Court's time for a few days in this matter when we could finish it in the next hour, and the jury returns a verdict of guilty, I will be minded to put a term of imprisonment on her, hear me?" I said I understood and we returned to court and the trial began.

We were very fortunate to have no less than six women on the jury. And when Teresa gave her statement from the dock, half the jury were crying. After the Judge summed up the case, the jury retired for only ten minutes and then returned a verdict of not guilty.

After the verdict, Teresa was acquitted and left the court with her family. The trial judge, as was the custom in those days, invited Victor Nunez and myself to his Chambers for a glass of sherry. Then is when I informed both of them what had caused Teresa to plead as she did. They were amazed, but the Judge did say: "I'll tell you truly this was the classic case of extreme provocation, I would have been shocked if the verdict was guilty."

Teresa became a very wealthy woman and I understand that she lived happily thereafter. I also know that she named the baby girl who was born in the Royal Gaol, 'Verna'.

Teresa Choon

CHAPTER 23

THE HOLY BIBLE AND TOBIAS

Sometime in 1984, my learned friend and colleague, Nizam Mohammed and I were retained to represent a man for malicious damage to property in the Tobago Assizes.

The case was set for trial on a Thursday, so we arrived in Tobago the day before and booked in at the Crown Reef Hotel and were given two rooms on the ground floor. Lovely rooms from which you could walk out on to the lawn and further on to the beach.

Anyway, the case started on the Thursday and lapped over to the Friday, when the jury retired and returned a verdict of not guilty. Everybody was happy about the result, and the accused's family insisted that they take Nizam and me to dinner that night. It was one of those cases where you really couldn't refuse. We had been booked to return to Trinidad, but the family arranged that we would return the Saturday instead.

We were taken to a lovely restaurant and after to a night club where there was music and dancing, and a floor show. This all ended at about midnight and then we were taken back to the Crown Reef Hotel. We thanked them for their hospitality and retired to our respective rooms after making arrangements for the front desk to call us at 6:30 am, so that we could catch the 9:00 am flight, on which we were booked, for Trinidad.

I had had a few too many to drink, so I had a shower and then lay down on the bed and said my prayers. Then I looked into the bedside cabinet and saw a Bible which I took out and began reading from page 1 until I fell asleep shortly after, with the Bible lying on my chest.

Sometime around 4:00 am, I awoke to see a big, big creole man about 6ft. 7in. tall, wearing only a bathing suit, standing over me with a long knife in his hand. I jumped like a kangaroo and landed on the side of the bed opposite him, and said: "Good morning Sir, I am Vernon De Lima. What is your name, and have you come to awaken me so that I will be on time for my flight?" We looked at each other for about a minute and then he said, with a deep, husky voice: "My name Tobias!"

I was so relieved, but I was real scared and said to him, "Then in that case, Mr. Tobias, it is a pleasure to meet you. Thank you for coming, let me show you the way out!" and I pointed to the glass door. He nodded and left.

I picked up the Bible which had fallen on the floor, secured the glass door by pushing a table up against it, and went back to sleep.

During the flight to Trinidad, I told Nizam what had happened and at first he didn't believe me. He could not understand how I failed to say anything about the incident to anybody at all, and to be honest, I didn't understand it either. It must have been that I had had quite a few the night before, and I was also extremely tired.

Anyway, when I arrived home I immediately telephoned the Crown Reef Hotel and spoke with the Manager. He told me that the man was a lunatic who escaped from police custody as arrangements were being made to transport him to St. Anns in Trinidad, but that he was apprehended in another guest's room after he left mine.

After that experience, I always had extra respect for the Holy Bible.

CHAPTER 24

POLICE AND 'TIEF' – WHO YOU 'FRAID MORE?

That is precisely how people in Trinidad and Tobago felt after experiencing Burroughs and his 'Flying Squad.' The public started distrusting the police, and for good reason. There were so many cases of police framing innocent people. The entire Police Service was turned upside down.

Mind you, there were still very many good police officers who stuck to their guns, and refused to allow Burroughs and his gang to influence them. But their fight was hard, very hard, and many of them looked forward to retirement rather than confrontation, because they well knew the cards were stacked against them, in every way.

I know that the Flying Squad spawned the officers involved in La Tinta. You could smell it a mile away. They thought they were a law unto themselves, and that could only have been so because they were made to believe that.

Just regard and consider what the Commissioners of the La Tinta Inquiry had cause to say about those police officers (ref: pgs. 90 & 91 *supra*), and in spite of that they were all re-instated in the service, and some of them promoted. And if you had any doubt, also consider the Dowd Report and the Scotland Yard Reports of 1992 and 1993, respectively. In both of those reports, the Police Service was painted as rotten.

We got to the stage where people were afraid to enter police stations for fear of how they would be treated.

I myself witnessed this, when one evening I had reason to visit the San Juan Police Station, because my client was being detained there. As I entered the Station, the young officer in the charge room looked at me and said, "What you come here for?" I was stunned and asked him if I was disturbing him. He simply repeated, "What you come here for?" I replied, "To make a report!" "About what?" he asked. "About you and your conduct!" I replied.

Just then the Sergeant on duty came out of the office and said, "Hey, Mr. De Lima, what can I do for you?" The young officer looked sheepishly at me, and I made it my business to let him know what he had done was very wrong. He apologized, but of course, the Sergeant was present and looking on.

So there it is, the public had over the years lost confidence in the police. People became afraid of them. It became widely felt, and still is, that if you witnessed a crime, the last thing you should do is make a report to the police. Because many of the policemen, not all mind you, but many are connected to the bandits.

This police criminal conduct permeated the entire judicial system. Policemen would not turn up to give evidence in cases, and exhibits would mysteriously disappear – sometimes being blamed on rodents – court transcripts would disappear, and sometimes even exhibits would change from the lower court to the Assizes: e.g., one bullet presented by the prosecution and marked as an exhibit in the Preliminary Inquiry, and a totally different one presented when the case came before the jury. It was unbelievable, but it happened in a case in San Fernando and a senior forensic expert was involved.

And there were some lawyers who not only condoned this type of behavior, but actually encouraged and promoted it. Thus, they came to be working hand-in-hand with the criminals.

Can you imagine what it took for a straightforward attorney to navigate himself/herself through that muck? There were many who just became so frightened and distraught they just refused to be associated with any criminal law matter. I know several attorneys who would never enter a criminal court in Trinidad precisely for those reasons.

It would be remiss of me not to say that there were many very good, honest and hardworking police officers in the service. But they became despondent and apprehensive for their good names and their families, and therefore opted for early retirement whenever possible.

I remember Mr. Osmond Kerr, Mr. Calvin Cox, Mr. Mayhew Alleyne, Mr. Joseph Lynch, Mr. Dyo Mohammed, Mr. Nadir Mohammed, Mr. Jim Wyse, Mr. Sanawah as being just a few of the many very honest and conscientious police officers I knew. When officers like those passed on, all hell broke loose in Trinidad and Tobago. And many of the decent ones well knew about the 'Flying Squad', the 'Kissoon Ramnannan Affair' and the 'La Tinta Affair' and were simply not prepared to expose themselves and their families to that type of danger.

Gary Griffith is a very good man, and I hope and pray that he will succeed in his job. But I am fearful for him because I have some idea what he is facing. He has to watch his back at all times. That is a matter of fact. And he will be well advised to remember the old people's saying: "All skin teeth ain't smile!"

Our Police Service has been the subject of investigation no

less than three times in the last thirty-five years. First, there was the Report of the La Tinta Commission of Enquiry – 1989. Then there was the O'Dowd Report of 1991, and then the Scotland Yard Report about Rodwell Murray and others and corruption in the T&T Police Service. *Each one of these reports describes our police service as dishonest, corrupt and dangerous.* But, until recently, when Gary Griffith was installed, nothing was done to deal with the situation. It is widely believed that the appointment to the post of Commissioner of Police in Trinidad and Tobago is dependent upon the political leaning of the applicant. If there is any doubt about that, the appointment will be one of 'Acting Commissioner', which appointment can be revoked at any time.

It is a fact that the certainty of punishment is far more important than the gravity of the punishment, because a person is more likely to avoid a crime if he is convinced that he will be caught. And he is more concerned about that than about how severe the punishment, should he be caught.

Corrupt police cause serious problems in the administration of justice in a country, and so it was in Trinidad in the eighties and nineties.

I remember the case of a young American girl who was caught attempting to leave Piarco on an American Airlines flight whilst transporting cocaine. She was a white girl and she was accompanied by a black girl who was also American. Both of them were transporting the drug but the police who made the arrest at Piarco allowed the black girl to fly out, even though the girl who was arrested kept protesting and saying that she had been commissioned by the black girl who was also carrying the drug. Again, the lead investigator in that case was a 'La Tinta Officer'.

You wouldn't believe that that would happen in Trinidad, but it did. When it does happen, the people involved lose all confidence in the belief that there is justice for all, and that is not good.

Because then, people feel forced to take the law into their own hands. In this case, the white American girl was given substantial bail and she absconded, never to be heard of again.

I later found out that the whole operation was a great farce to enhance the position of the local police investigator. That he had arranged with his illegal contacts in the USA to have these two girls travel to Trinidad, ostensibly to take 10 kilos of cocaine back to New York, and that thereby two things would be achieved: (1) he would arrest one girl in Trinidad, and (2) the other girl would successfully deliver her lot to his connections in the USA, with the blessing of the corrupt police there.

About ten years ago, there was a murder that took place in Trinidad in the west. A prominent man was assassinated outside his home. A person who lived nearby saw the killers, but was afraid to report it. He said that one of the killers was a senior police officer who knocked on his door and asked him if he saw anything.

There is where our Police Service had reached.

CHAPTER 25

POLITICS AND ME

Jennifer wanted us to leave Trinidad since 2008. Our children had all gone, and it was her wish to be with them in our old age. So I kept promising her that it would be soon. She detested politics and the PNM and the UNC political parties, both of which she distrusted. I assured her I was putting things in place to go. I stopped taking new cases and really was trying my best to scale down.

However, one morning, my driver Ram Sookoo, took me to the Tunapuna Magistrates' Court for a case that was at least two years old and had not even started. Each time I appeared the Police sought an adjournment for one reason or another, and it was always granted.

This time was no different. When the case was called, I announced that I was ready to proceed and once more the Police prosecutor said they were not and asked for yet another adjournment. I couldn't believe what I was hearing and right away said, "Your Worship, this case is two years old and the Prosecution is never ready. We always are. I ask that you discharge my client!" Whereupon, Her Worship said, "No, Mr. De Lima, I will adjourn this matter!" She then put it to a date nine months later.

I bowed and packed my briefcase and got up to leave, when the Magistrate said, "Mr. De Lima, you are smiling. May I ask you why?" I responded: "Madam, our country is in peril. And I verily believe that when the justice system becomes clogged and courts keep adjourning and adjourning cases without good reason, it is not a good thing. It will only end bad."

She responded: "Well, Mr.De Lima, you may think what you wish, but this is my court and I will decide when and how to grant adjournments." I then said, "I understand Madam. Now, may I take my leave?" She said that I could, and I left.

I was not only angry, but I felt distraught. What did all this mean? I intended to go right home and tell Jennifer that I had decided we should leave Trinidad right away.

However, as we were proceeding down Pasea Main Road Ram said to me, "Boss, look Mr. Winston Dookeran there!" I didn't have a clue what he was talking about, and so I asked who he was. Ram said, "He's the leader of the new political party they talking about!" I said, "Stop the car!" And I got out and walked over to where Mr. Dookeran was and introduced myself. He invited me into his office which was across the road and we spoke for about two hours. I joined the party that afternoon and was given a card stating: Member of The Congress of The People.

I have always been intrigued by politics but I myself never wished to be a politician. But the situation in Trinidad had become so bad that I thought I should at least try to help instead of simply leaving. The PNM was a bad Government and Prime Minister Manning was doing as he pleased. Everybody was fed up at the time.

The two political parties in Trinidad and Tobago are really the same. They seem to have an arrangement of appeasement between themselves. And irrespective of the suffering of the people they are content to soldier on – 'One term for you and the next term for me!'

I was very impressed and still am with Mr. Winston Dookeran and the tenets he espoused, and so I decided that I would throw in my lot with him. Problem was, I still had to convince Jennifer.

So I invited Winston and his dear wife Shirley to our home for dinner and Jenny loved them right away.

From then on, I became a spokesman for the C.O.P. and I was so proud of it. When the first election came on in November 2007 the COP got 184,000 votes but did not win even one seat. The P.N.M. won again with a small majority. Winston was very upset, but I was sure it was only a matter of time before we would prevail.

So said, within two and a half years of the PNM victory, the Calder Hart scandal arose. He was an Englishman who held so many very important posts given to him by the Manning PNM Government, but he was himself corrupt and stole millions from Trinidad.

Everybody was talking about this, and Timothy Hamel-Smith and I kept pounding at Manning about Hart and what he had done, until he, Manning, was virtually forced to call an election.

When the election took place on the 16th of April 2010, the Peoples Partnership Coalition won. This was a coalition of the UNC and the COP. The UNC had won twenty one seats and the COP six. The PNM managed to win only fourteen. It was a proper 'cut ass'. I called it a 'cutasstrophy'.

Our successful candidates were: Winston Dookeran (Tunapuna), Carolyn Seepersad Bachan (San Fernando West), Lincoln Douglas (Lopinot/Bonaire West), Prakash Ramadhar (St. Augustine), Roger Samuel (Arima) and Anil Roberts (D'Abadie/O'Meara).

We were delighted and everybody looked forward to at last having a good government which would ensure fairness and all round propriety and respect for all our citizens. There was a fresh breeze blowing, a feeling of joy, and also a feeling of goodwill for all the people. Both Jennifer and I were so happy that we were going to be involved in turning our country around, so that all our citizens would experience relief from the Manning Government and the iniquity it had spawned over the years.

People hailed us in the road and wished us well, and I felt so proud that we were being of some good use to the people of Trinidad and Tobago. It was the greatest time of my life. I felt I was helping to make the lives of all Trinidadians and Tobagonians better. I thought that now, everybody would be given a fair opportunity to make a good living, and so crime would definitely go down rapidly. I used to go around humming Bro Valantino's tune: *Trinidad is nice, Trinidad is a Paradise.*

When ministerial positions were being considered, without consulting me, Winston put my name forward for the post of Minister of National Security, but Jack Warner proposed Mr John Sandy and he was appointed. I was pleased, because I never wished to be appointed, and I felt sure Mr Sandy would do a good job.

But, within two to three months, everything changed.

I had been given a job by the Partnership to be an Intermediary between the public and the Government. An office was assigned to me in Flagship House COP Headquarters in Broome Street, Woodbrook, and I would receive people three times a week from 12:00 noon until 5:00 pm. I had the telephone number of every one of our members of Parliament, and could and would call them if I needed to. And I had a wonderful secretary, Ms. Francis Hamel-Smith, who is now deceased and who was indispensable to me. She was just the best. In fact, for what she put up with in Flagship House, I am sure she is a Saint in Heaven.

I interviewed a few hundred people and was able to assist some of them. But as time went by, I got the feeling that I was being ignored. That my job was irrelevant.

One day, a very gentle man came to see me and explained that he was a small contractor and had done a job for the Manning Government six months before the election and he had not yet been paid. It was, he explained, not a very big job, and his bill was $95,000.00, but he needed the money because otherwise he would lose his eight workmen that were threatening to leave him.

I took his statement, and immediately Francis called the Line Minister, who happened to be Mr. Roodal Moonilal. I had never met him before but I said, "Morning, Minister. This is De Lima from Flagship. How are you doing?" And then I told him about the man and his problem.

His response to me was, "De Lima, that man is a member of the PNM. We won the election. Let him wait. Don't take them kind a people on!" I said that I thought we won the election to represent all the people; not only the people of the UNC and COP. He then said, "Like you didn't hear me?" I said thanks and put down the phone. I looked at the man sitting in front of me and apologized. I was mortified. I didn't know what to do. We had promised that we would be the Government for all the people, not just for the Coalition. We lied to the country.

A few days after, I asked for a meeting with Mr. Dookeran. I met with him and told him what happened with that small contractor. It was by that time clear to me that the UNC thought they were in charge and there was nothing we could do or say about it. I reminded Mr. Dookeran what we had promised the people on the campaign and suggested to him that we demit the Coalition on a matter of principle.

He said to me that we were in Government and so had a responsibility to the Government, to which I responded by pointing out that we really had no place in that Government if what we stood for was being totally ignored. That for us to stay on would be a betrayal of the confidence the voters had placed in us. I also said to him that I was convinced if we stood our ground on principle, the people would elect the COP resoundingly when the next election came up.

As a result of our conversation, Mr. Dookeran called a meeting of all six of our members of Parliament to meet with the COP Executive. Only two attended, Winston and Carolyn. It was clear then that the other four had decided they were not interested in jeopardizing their positions with the Coalition Government and would continue on as ministers.

It was then clear to me the COP had capitulated. But I went a step further. I caused an executive meeting to be called at which I put forward my proposal that we demit the Coalition. It was put to a vote and I lost 38 to 9. As a result of my defeat, I resigned immediately and never attended another meeting. That was how politics ended for me.

I do not regret my experience with the COP and politics. It was a great time for me, because I had some degree of hope while it lasted. I must say though that I learnt that in politics there are more dirty and corrupt people than you can ever meet in a criminal court. It's like flies to honey. The most brilliant men and women are prepared to lie and conspire and betray other people, some of whom may even be their friends, in order to get on politically.

Irrespective of their family reputations or religious or professional affiliations, they would do the damnedest things to position themselves so that they would be part of the government. It amazed and frightened me. I therefore give you, my reader, this advice: *Beware of Politicians. Don't trust them until you have known them at least ten years.*

Jennifer had long before lost confidence in the COP. It happened during the COP Internal Election for Political Leader which I contested. During that campaign we saw members of the UNC wearing COP jerseys at our meetings and openly supporting Prakash Ramadhar. She resigned at once, and never even wanted to talk a word of politics again.

That is not to say I didn't meet good people in politics. I did. For years, every Friday a group of concerned Trinidadians would meet at 7:00 am at the Normandie Hotel, under the Chairmanship of the great Mr. Fred Chin Lee, whom we called 'the Chairman of the Board.'

The persons who met there met as Trinidadians, and not as members of any political party. Fred was a giant of a man whose only interest was the betterment of Trinidad and Tobago.

Among the persons I was privileged to see at these breakfast meetings were Selby Wilson, Robert Mayers, Reggie Dumas, David Abdullah, Winston Dookeran, Morgan Jobe, Ronald Huggins, Wendy Lee Yuen, Mariano Brown, Hoolsie Bhagan, Louis Lee Sing and many more.

Thank you Fred, and may God bless you and yours.

I left politics as I met politics. Sadly, I was not able to do a positive thing in politics, other than help to bring down the PNM Manning Government in 2010. But to what avail, I often ask.

I am certain that there is a third constituency in the politics in Trinidad and Tobago. I call it the 'Third Force'. It comprises people who want the best for Trinidad and Tobago, but they will not vote for either the PNM or the UNC.

These folks will not vote for either because they do not respect those parties. And this third force comprises people from every ethnic group. I really feel that the day some good citizen is able to impress them, he or she will form the Government that will bring our beloved Trinidad and Tobago back on track.

I shall always believe that the COP had that chance, and threw it away – "How sad. Too bad!"

The people of Trinidad and Tobago will get fed up one day and then all will be fixed. I feel certain that I will not live to see it, but it will happen. I promise you it will. Mark my words.

CHAPTER 26

THE AWARD OF SILK – A TRINIDAD DISGRACE

That award is a total farce now. And it became so since Independence 1962. The Governments since then have made it a farce. They would give that accolade, which by then was known as 'Senior Counsel', to their own people, and others who supported them, or with whom they were pleased, irrespective of whether the recipients ever even entered a Court of Law.

I practiced in the criminal courts since 1966 and I thought I was doing o.k. I never had time to even consider taking 'silk'.

Sometime around 1990, my Senior, Mr. Bruce Procope, Q.C. summoned me to his office one day and said that he thought it was time for me to apply for silk. I was so happy and delighted and felt honored. I thanked him and went home and discussed it with Jennifer. We agreed that I should apply and I did. A few weeks later the silk announcements were made and I was not among them. I said nothing and continued on my professional journey.

Again, around 2002, I received a telephone call from a gentleman who explained that he was attached to the A.G.s Department, and that he was instructed to call me and invite me to apply for silk.

I told him what happened the first time I applied, and he assured me that there would be no recurrence of that experience. Once more my wife and I discussed it and once again, with her approval, I filled out the form and submitted it.

Two weeks later the appointments were announced, and I was not among them.

Jennifer said to me, "Vernon. We have been married for thirty-six years and I have never said anything like this to you before. If you ever apply for silk again I will leave you! Do you understand me?" I said that I did and I wouldn't lie, I was scared – more from what she had said.

So, no question of the S.C. ever arose again until the end of 2011. The Coalition Government was in office, and I was invited to apply once again. I had great difficulty in convincing my dear wife, but she relented and I applied. This time I was among the appointees.

But the whole process that year was marred because for the first time, two High Court judges were also appointed senior counsel. There was great protest by members of the legal profession, and the judges, who really should have known better, were forced to return their silk appointments. To make matters worse, the Prime Minister, Mrs Kamla Persad Bissessar had absolutely no compunction in appointing herself as Senior Counsel. The whole process was thereby demeaned. Sad but true.

As I have always understood it, the award of silk is made to attorneys who have excelled in their practice at the bar. It is that simple, but as I said earlier, the appointments became a political matter over the years, thus marring the whole very important matter of being elevated to the Inner Bar. What a mess! It was 'curry favour and friend' and in and between a deserving person would be appointed, to make the process appear above board.

A few months after I was appointed Senior Counsel, I had occasion to meet the Prime Minister in a party in the Rienzi Complex in Couva. I hadn't seen her for over a year and she appeared very ebullient and high-spirited. I paid my respects to her and was about to move on when she leaned across to me and said, "Mr. De Lima. My dear Mr. De Lima. My dear, dear Mr. De Lima. I worked so hard to convince my colleagues to give you silk, and up to today you have never written to me nor even said thanks for what I did!"

I was so taken aback by her remark, I replied, "My dear Prime Minister, I did not think I had to thank anyone for receiving that appointment!" I left the function and I have never seen her since.

I thought it only right that I should share that experience because it shows clearly what 'Taking Silk' has become in Trinidad and Tobago. For decades it has been nothing more than a farce.

And I feel very much for so many very good advocates who were never even considered for the silk appointment over the years I was there. Counsel such as Nizam Mohammed, Joseph Pantor, Nathaniel King, Wayne Sturge, Ravi Rajkummar, Clive Phelps, and so many others.

The whole process was and still is so unfair that it is rotten. I well remember when my dear friend and colleague, Trevor Lee, was appointed Senior Counsel he told the newspapers, "Now is when they give this to me? When I am about to retire?" That said it all.

And what was clear was that as soon as certain attorneys were elevated to the status of Senior Counsel, they shut their mouths and totally discarded their colleagues who were unfairly denied that elevation over and over and over. Why? Just one word! GREED! Many of them knew that they were in no way comparable to those that had been refused the accolade, but they said not one damn word about it. And in some cases, persons of dubious character were given 'SILK'. The attitude was: I'm all right, Jack!

And yet they continue to call one another 'My Learned Friend'. In that case, you may well ask, 'Who the hell needs a Learned Enemy?' I feel no compunction whatsoever about relating this because it is so manifestly unfair and it has caused so much rancor, and even hatred, in our profession, that it has to be addressed *statim*. It offends against the very words of our National Anthem. And there is such hypocrisy. If a Senior member of the profession should die, they all line up to bestow accolades on him even though 'they pissed on him' all during his life.

As a result of all this, *GRAVITAS* no longer obtains in our profession in Trinidad and Toabgo. Sad but absolutely true. Mitra must be turning in his grave, for he fought so hard for 'Counsel' to be respected in Trinidad and Tobago. That is Mr. Mitra Sinanan, Q.C.

I hope the day will come again when such appointments will be fair and meritorious. It may not seem important, but I promise you that it is another cog in the wheel of the judicial system that was politically interfered with to the detriment of the profession, and ultimately, to the judicial system itself.

CHAPTER 27

THE MAGISTRATE AND THE BUSINESSMAN

As a legal practitioner, I would go from court to court all over the Island. In 1987, Patrick Jagassar was the Senior Magistrate attached to the Chaguanas Magistrates' Court in Chaguanas. He was highly respected and had been on the bench for a number of years before being assigned to Chaguanas.

Bhola Nandlal was a young, bright, and resourseful businessman from Bejucal road in Cunupia. He was an importer of ground provision goods such as carrots, potatoes and the like. He had done very well for himself.

Bhola was charged with possession of an unlicensed firearm. He was stopped in a police road block, and the firearm was discovered in his car.

When he appeared in the Chaguanas Magistrates' Court, the presiding magistrate was Mr. Patrick Jagassar. Attorney for Bhola was an ex-Police Inspector.

Someone told Bhola that the magistrate Jagasser was sympathetic, but that firearm offences were very serious and people guilty of such offences should be given prison sentences of no less than one year at first instance. But that he, Jagassar, being an understanding and compassionate person, would ensure that Bhola would escape gaol if he did the following: (1) Make arrangements for a Toyota Royal Saloon motor car be delivered in the name of Patrick Jagassar, and (2) Pay the sum of TT $100,000.00 in cash to him, Jagassar.

Bhola thought about what he was told and decided that he needed to be clear of the law because he was doing so very well in business he would pay what the magistrate wanted. In his simplicity he never realized that doing so would involve him in a most serious crime. Accordingly, arrangements were made and Bhola paid for the car and ensured that the $100,000.00 was delivered. And then he was found not guilty by Jagassar and discharged.

But there was a serious catch. Sitting as Magistrate in the Chaguanas 2nd Magistrates' Court, was a bold, forthright and honest man called Algernon Jack. He was not liked because he was stringent. He was a fair magistrate, but he was brutal when he found you guilty. And I fear that is what we needed then but need even more today.

Anyway, it was he, Jack, who was able to put a stop to Jagassar and what he was doing in the 1st Court for a couple of years. He reported to the police what was happening in the court next to his and they commenced investigations.

Bhola was charged that on the 22nd December 1986, he gave a car, a Toyota Royal Saloon, valued $102,195.00 to Patrick Jagassar, as a gift or reward for dismissing criminal charges against him at the Chaguanas Magistrates' Court. He was also charged for giving Patrick Jagassar $100,000.00 as an inducement.

Both Bhola Nandlal and Patrick Jagassar were arrested and criminally charged. One for GIVING the bribe and the other for TAKING the bribe. I was retained to represent Bhola and I went to the D.P.P. and asked him to accept Bhola as a witness against Patrick. He refused.

In May 1988, Jagassar and Nandlal went on trial in the Port of Spain 2nd Assize Court before Mr. Justice Anthony Lucky. They were found guilty and sentenced to two years imprisonment with hard labor.

On one of the days of their trial, all the parties and their respective counsels were standing outside the court in the Hall of Justice at a lunchtime break, when Bhola said to me, "Mr. De Lima. Look there is Patrick across the hall. Please go and ask him to return the $100,000.00 I gave him."

I walked over to where Jagassar was standing and I told him what Nandlal had said, to which he replied, "Mr. De Lima, I am afraid Mr. Nandlal does not understand. I requested certain things to ensure that Mr. Nandlal would be discharged. I was given those things – a motor car and a sum of money. He paid and I delivered. Thereafter, I found him not guilty. The contract was fulfilled. I owe him absolutely nothing!"

Bhola died a few years after he came out of prison and his three sons now run his business in Chaguanas. To my mind Bhola Nandlal was one of the worse cases of discrimination. Imagine. Bhola offers to testify for the State and the State refuses. The Magistrate is the State's Officer. Bhola is just a nobody who is coerced and finds himself in Holy Hell.

I feel so sorry whenever I recount this event. Because it manifests the inequity of our society. Here is a good young man. But because he is wealthy, he is lured into a web by persons who conspire to fleece him. And yet the State could not bring itself to understand this and to offer amnesty to Bhola. If ever there was a deserving case it was this one. The Almighty knows.

But to be fair, Mr. Patrick Jaggasar has repented and is today highly respected. He is a good man and his impact on Trinidad will surely be felt very soon. Pat, I salute you!

CHAPTER 28

THE INFLUENCE OF HOLLYWOOD ON CRIME

Sad to say, but movies have a great influence on societies all over the world. What is more, many of the prominent movie figures understand that very well, and employ their popularity to persuade people politically.

I remember well when I was a teenager. The movie stars then were confined (or confined themselves) to acting, looking handsome and beautiful, and sexy, and generally influencing global society by how they behaved.

Bob Hope and Bing Crosby and Frank Sinatra and Fred Astaire and Louis Armstrong and Nat King Cole and Elizabeth Taylor and Hedy Lamarr and Mahalia Jackson and Billie Holiday were some of those stars. They entertained the world, but they left politics to others.

Not so today. Movie stars nowadays feel that it is their given right and privilege to have political influence at all times. And not only are many of them and their films puerile and really stupid, but many others are dangerous. I say dangerous because I have actually experienced the consequence of one such film.

Many years ago, I was retained by a family to represent a young man for murder. The allegation was that he and two other men had murdered a man in the Couva area. There were originally four men charged, but one decided to turn and give evidence for the State against the other three.

The State's case was that on a particular day these four young men kidnapped a man in Chaguanas and handcuffed him and put him to sit in the front seat next to the driver; and that whilst they were transporting him through the cane fields of Couva, one of them who was sitting in the back seat put a piano wire around the victim's neck and vigorously pulled it. The man was decapitated. My client said that they had seen that act performed in a Robert De Niro movie a few days before. That movie was named *Goodfellas*.

Fortunately for me, I did not have to do the trial because my client died before the case came on.

We live in a different world from what I knew growing up, and I understand that. But basic values, such as honesty, respect and compassion seem to be no more. I hope I am wrong about this, but I really don't think I am. The recent fiasco at the Oscars involving Will Smith appears to prove my point.

CHAPTER 29

I DEFEND A CREEP

This is a story that just has to be told. It's importance will become evident.

The kidnapping and murders of young girls in Trinidad started in the 1980s. There was the case of a young Indian girl named Shakantullah who disappeared and was later found dead in Caroni. Her body was found floating in a lagoon in the middle of a cane field.

Just around that time, Juliet Tam, a young school teacher who lived in Arima, disappeared and has never been found. She left her home going for an exercise run and was never seen again. This case affected all parents in Trinidad and my daughter Krysta was friendly with her sister Fleur, who was in her class at St Augustine Girls High School.

Around the same time, I was retained to represent a Hindu Pundit who was charged for the murder of a young woman in the Caroni area. The person who retained me was the Pundit's father-in-law, who I called Baba. He was a good and gentle man.

The allegation was that he the Pundit followed a young woman who was driving her car along the Southern Main Road, and at some point he purposely bounced her car from behind in order to get her to stop. Thereafter he persuaded her to come into his car so that they could go to the Police Station to report the accident. She was never again seen alive.

I took instructions from the Pundit and was very impressed with him and what he said. I even thought that he was very unfortunate to have been in that area at the time and that he had been so unlucky to have been charged. To me, it was a simple case, and I had no doubt he would be acquitted.

The case was heard in the P.O.S. 1st Assize Court in the Red House and there were at least fifty Hindu Pundits in the Court, following the trial. They were there to see and hear exactly what was being alleged. Understandably.

In those days I was a smoker, so when the jury retired to consider their verdict, I walked onto the western verandah of the Red House and lit up and smoked and smoked. You know how. After about an hour of smoking, waiting for the jury's verdict, Baba came up to me and said, "Mr. De Lima, what you think? Will he get off?"

I felt so happy to say to him, "Baba, don't worry yourself, the jury will find him not guilty."

What happened next left me in a state of shock. Baba said to me, "Oh God, No! Don't tell me that! Sir, we didn't want you to win this case. We paid you to defend him. That was a show. But we didn't want you to win the case."

I said, "So you paid me to lose the case?"

Then he said, "Sir, he really kill the woman!"

I was stunned and feebly asked, "How you know that?"

He replied, "My daughter, his wife, told me that she washed his clothes when he came home that night and that they were all covered in blood."

Shortly after this conversation the Jury returned a verdict of not guilty and the priest was discharged. I wrote a précis of our conversation and delivered it to the authorities, but nothing further was ever heard of it. I was not surprised.

For years, I could never understand why the wife would do as Baba said. But one day, whilst fishing five miles outside Trinidad, my fishing partner said to me, "Boss, a Hindu husband is regarded as a GOD in a household. He can do no wrong."

I said, "Even if he murders another woman and the crime is sexual?" He replied, "Even so!"

When I got back home I told Jenny about my conversation in the boat with Sankar and she said, "Well, I ain't know 'bout Hindu, but if you did that I would lock up your ass so fast, you wouldn't know what hit you!" Strange eh? What does all that tell you about our beloved country?

About two years after this case, I was going into Hi Lo[6] St. Augustine one morning when a man sitting in a car called out to me, "How's the boss?" I looked and realized it was the Priest. I walked across to him and said, "When I come out of Hi Lo, if you are still here, I will call the Police!" He drove off and I never saw him again. I heard that he was killed in a car accident a few years later.

---

6. Hi Lo is a supermarket chain in Trinidad

CHAPTER 30

NANKISSOON BOODRAM aka DOLE CHADEE

Sometime in 1990, I was representing a man called Russel Ramdhanie for an assault case in the Tunapuna Magistrates' Court. Russel lived in Bamboo Village, Curepe, and he knew everybody who lived there or near there. From time to time he would bring people to me who were charged by the police. It was purely voluntary on his part; there was absolutely no lawyer-tout relationship between us.

One day Russel said to me that he knew a man called Dole Chadee who was in trouble with the police and needed a good lawyer. He asked me if I would see him, and I agreed. A meeting was set up and Dole came and met with me at my home 'Outdoor Office' which adjoined my home. This was structured in the way my dear and renowned friend Mr. Malcolm Butt, Q.C. had advised me many years before.

Chadee explained to me that he had retained a lawyer in San Fernando to represent him, but that he was dissatisfied with him because he (Chadee) did not respect him.

I asked him what he meant, and this was his explanation. He said that two members of his family were charged for possession of cocaine in the Princes Town Magistrates' Court and there was only one civilian witness the police were calling, and that his lawyer had advised him to make arrangements to pay the witness to change his evidence – in that way ensuring the discharge of his relatives. Chadee said he told the lawyer that he had paid him a large sum of money and that if that was the way to win the case then he the lawyer should pay the witness out of his fee. Of course, the lawyer refused.

I was stunned. I looked at him for a good two minutes before I spoke. Then I said, "You lie!" He said, "I'm not lying, Sir!" Thereafter, he severed relations with the lawyer who I must say never forgave him, up to the day he was hanged. That was my introduction to this man whom I represented on several occasions.

People have asked me so many questions about Dole Chadee over the years. I knew him as a client and that was that. As I explained earlier, an attorney is obliged to represent anyone who requires his services 'zealously within the bounds of the law'. That is the lawyer's duty, but it is also the client's right. That principal has to be always understood and respected.

I think that representing Dole Chadee in his many cases was a learning lesson for me. I learnt that people are greedy for power and wealth, and that they would murder to achieve them. I also learned that in a society like Trinidad's, there are always people who are not afraid to take advantage of other people so as to prosper unlawfully. I experienced this on a number of occasions. A wealthy person would contact me and say, "Represent Jack Bando and just send me the bill!"

In representing Chadee, I got to realise that 'all was not well in the State of Trinidad' and that the entire Police, Judicial and Penal systems were broken, and it would be most difficult, if not impossible, to salvage them.

What is more, I began to understand, with a degree of horror, that some of the most 'respected' people in our society were, in fact, rogues and vagabonds of the highest order. Many of them were often in the society columns in the newspaper, with their wives and associates. When asked how they became so wealthy in so short a period of time, their response would be that they made their money in the USA Stock Market, or that they won the Power Ball Lottery, or that they inherited it from a relative who died in Europe. And these people were able to get away with it.

Parts of Trinidad were identified as being where the 'Untouchables' lived. St Clair is one such place. Valsayn is another. Federation Park, Ellersie Park, Westmoorings and St. Joseph Village too, and several others in the country and in the deep south.

There were so many very strange cases that came before the courts, and so many others that took years to reach the courts, that they have thrown a web of serious doubt over our entire system. I feel sorry for many of the Judges, because they have to see and know what is happening, and can do or say absolutely nothing about it.

Over fifty firearms (including machine guns and semi-automatic rifles) were found in a house in Valsayn. A billion dollars worth of cocaine were found in a water tank on a vacation property on Monos Island. Millions of dollars worth of cocaine were found in fruit juice tins shipped from Trinidad to the USA, and there were many others – and there was no proper resolution. In the case of the cocaine on Monos Island, five "Peewats" (poor boys who didn't even own a car) were convicted and sent to prison for a very long time. Even the trial judge lamented that she was convinced the real big men were not caught.

It is in that setting that Dole Chadee existed. Randolph Burroughs was in his heyday and the Flying Squad henchmen reigned supreme, and cocaine had arrived on the scene. Before that, the cases were mostly of marijuana, which to be truthful, I always considered a 'peaceful' drug, akin to alcohol. I myself never smoked it because of an experience I had in England when I was a student there. A good friend of mine, Tony, who was from Trinidad and was there studying law as well, used to smoke marijuana (weed) and from time to time when he came from Birmingham (where he was studying) to London he would stay in my digs (rented room) and sleep on the extra bed there. And he would smoke marijuana in the room. And I would leave the room because it made me feel nauseous, and one night I actually vomited. I never forgot the smell of marijuana – a sickening 'burning bush' smell.

But to each his own. It is now becoming legal all over and I have no doubt it will be legal in Trinidad soon. In fact, it is legal to have a small quantity.

Mr. Procope and I represented Dole Chadee and his family in several cases over the years and we always found him to be a person of his word. If he told you something it was always the truth. In May 1994, Dole Chadee and eight other men were arrested and charged for murdering an entire family in Piparo on the 10th of January 1994.

The accused were Nankissoon Boodram (aka Dole Chadee), Joey Ramiah, Ramkellewan Singh, Clive Thomas, Robin Gopaul, Russel Sankerali, Levi Morris, Joel Ramsingh, Stephen Eversley and Bhagwandee Singh.

Their trial began on the 26th of July 1996 in a special court in Chaguaramas, presided over by Mr. Justice Lionel Jones, a gentleman of the highest order.

Appearing for the State were Mr. Timothy Cassels, Q.C. (from England), Mr. Theodore Guerra, S.C., Mr. Mark Mohammed (DPP) and Ms. Gillian Lucky.

Appearing for Chadee and the other men were Mr. Ronald Thwaites, Q.C. (from England), Mr. Desmond Allum, S.C., Mr. Frank Solomon, S.C. Mr. Prakash Ramadhar, Mr. Joseph Pantor, Mr. Ravi Rajkammar, Mr. Jagdeo Singh, and me, Vernon De Lima.

On the very first day of the trial, the lead attorney for the State, Mr. Cassels, Q.C. announced to the Court that accused number six, Levi Morris, would be pleading guilty to the offences charged, and that he had been granted a Presidential pardon and would be giving evidence for the State.

The trial lasted just under six weeks, and they were all convicted on the 3rd of September 1996 and sentenced to death.

I was, and am still of the opinion, that the nine accused made a grave error by not giving evidence at their trial. But, say what. It was their choice, individually.

On the 16th of May 1997, their appeals were dismissed by the Court of Appeal of Trinidad and Tobago. Thereafter, the nine appealed to the Privy Council and their appeals were dismissed on the 26th of May 1999.

On Friday the 4th of June 1999, Dole Chadee, Joey Ramiah and Ramkellewan Singh were hanged at the Royal Gaol.

On the following day, Saturday, Clive Thomas, Robin Gopaul and Russel Sankerali were executed.

For some reason there was a rest day on the Sunday, and on Monday the 7th, the remaining three, Joel Ramsingh, Stephen Eversley and Bhagwandeen Singh were hanged.

Trinidad was traumatized. Even the prison officers were affected. Some of them were obliged to take medical leave and counselling. It was a serious time. But I well remember that for at least two months after the hangings, the murder rate went dramatically down to about one-fifth of what it usually was. I am now firmly an advocate for the retention of the death penalty.

Three days before Dole was executed, I went to see him in the condemned cells. I sat with him and we spoke. Just before I left he said this to me, "Sir, I want to tell you something. I agree with the death penalty!" I was quite taken aback. I said goodbye and left the prison.

The society in Trinidad and Tobago is so corrupt that persons like Dole Chadee seem meek. As I said before, the rich and affluent do whatever they like and get away with it. Why is that? Simple, they are protected. By whom? That is the number one question.

Point as they like at Dole Chadee, he was not the cause of the decay. Some of the big shots of our society should be man enough to stand up and claim that prize. For they damn well know of whom I speak. Many of them rent the front pews of the churches, and are conspicuously present in them on Sundays.

Dole Chadee and me

CHAPTER 31

OUR WONDERFUL STAFF IN CHAMBERS

An important reason for the success of our Chambers was undoubtedly the quality of our employees. No business can ever be very successful without very good employees, and it is a pity that more attention is not given to this fact.

In our case we were blessed with having four of the most accomplished and kind people working for us. Mrs. Phyllis Rickhi, Mr. Clyde Gadjadhar, Mr. Eddie Mahipat and Mr. Roodal Maharaj were those four.

When I entered the Chambers in 1965, I met all four of them there. And it is to them that I attribute a great part of whatever success I attained in the profession. They were always there for me and on many occasions they guided me along the right path.

They were experienced people, two of them having actually worked with Sir Lennox O'Reilly, K.C. and his brother Guy O'Reilly, Q.C. And I learnt quickly there is no substitute for experience in any profession. They are all deceased now, but I shall never forget how good they were to me, and to all the other young lawyers who were fortunate enough to be in those Chambers.

CHAPTER 32

HANS BOOS, EX-CURATOR OF THE ZOO

Hans is my wife Jennifer's first cousin. From a young man, he was interested in wildlife and what comes with it. He kept various reptiles as pets, and over the years became one of the world's leading authorities on snakes about which he has written two books. He is an international authority on venomous snakes.

In addition, he worked as curator of the Zoo in Melbourne, Australia for a number of years before taking up the job of curator of the Emperor Valley Zoo on the northern side of the Queens Park Savannah in Port of Spain. However, snakes and wild life were not his only interest. He was an avid collector of materials of all types. He collected comic books and boasted that he had full collections of the Superman and Batman and Mutt and Jeff comic books. And he did have them.

Unfortunately, he also collected pornographic material. It was, he said, among his collectable hobbies. On the 29th of June 1993, Hans was arrested by the Police at his home in the Zoo and charged for possession of pornographic material. This consisted of many photographs and DVD movies and tapes.

Mr. Gilbert Peterson and I were retained to represent him. We argued that in Trinidad and Tobago it was not unlawful for a person to have pornographic material in his possession for his personal use. We succeeded and Hans was discharged. But it took nearly two years before that decision was given in 1995.

One year later, on the 4th of February 1996, Hans was arrested in Miami as he arrived on a BWIA flight from Trinidad.

I well remember the day he was arrested. I was driving my car on my way home at about 4:00 pm when I heard the news on the radio. It was quite a shock for me, because a few months before he had asked me if I thought it was all right for him to travel to the States, and I recall telling him that I thought it was not a good idea. He also checked with Peterson who agreed with my advice. So, it struck me that he had acted contrary to what we had both advised.

However, when I got home that afternoon, I told Jennifer what I had heard on the radio and she went very silent. After a few minutes she said: "I advised him to go! He telephoned here yesterday to speak with you and as you were out at the time he explained to me what he wished to speak to you about. He told me he was invited by an American friend of his who was a lecturer at a University in Illinois to lecture to the West Indian students there how to make local things like Chee Kee Chong and Mad Bull kites and Bobbin tractors, etc. I told him I thought it was a noble thing to do and that he should definitely go." That made sense. I walked away and went to shower.

Hans was tried and convicted in the USA and sentenced to five years imprisonment. However, he was a model prisoner and lectured to the other prisoners about snakes and other venomous creatures After thirty months, he was discharged and deported to Trinidad.

Hans Boos died in Trinidad last year and is still considered one of the leading world authorities of wildlife, particularly snakes.

Contrary to what appeared recently in the newspapers, Hans Boos was never charged with child pornography of any sort.

CHAPTER 33

DANGEROUS TRINIDAD

I shall always love Trinidad and Tobago, but I recognize that it is a very dangerous place today.

On the morning of Saturday the 21st March 2015, Jennifer and I were attacked by two men in our property where we had lived peacefully for fifty years.

At about 5:45 am, I was asleep in our bedroom upstairs of our property in St. Augustine. Jennifer got out of bed when she heard the dogs barking, and without awaking me, she turned off the burglar alarm and went downstairs and out the back door to try to calm the dogs.

As soon as she went outside the house, a man jumped on her and threw her to the ground, and began kicking her with his steel tipped boots (which she heard when he was running toward her) until she passed out. We believe they left her for dead and then proceeded into our home and up the stairs to our bedroom.

One of the dogs kept licking her face, and she awoke and crawled on all fours to the back door and into a toilet downstairs, where she locked the door and sat on the floor. By that time, she could hear the noises from upstairs where they were engaging me.

I was awakened by two men with bandanas over their faces standing over my bed. One of them was holding a silver revolver in his hand and they were shouting at me, "Don't make any noise, get out the bed!" I got up off the bed and the man with the firearm (whom I call the Leader) hit me on my head with it and kept saying, "Where the focking gun. We want the gun!" I replied that I had no gun. Then the other man opened the drawer next to my bed and found my firearm. The leader said, "For lying, take this!" And he hit me again with his gun. Then he said, "Lay down on the floor!" I refused and said I had just recently had a hip replacement, whereupon he kicked me in the area of my hip, saying, "That's for your focking hip!" The other man kept shouting, "Shoot him now! Shoot him, shoot him!"

Then the Leader said: "We want money. Where the focking money?" I replied that we didn't keep money in the house but that I did have some in my office which adjoined the bedroom. They then ripped a gold chain with a miraculous medal from my neck and dragged me into my office and put me to sit in my office chair. I pointed to a law book into which I had put $350.00 the day before. The Leader became furious and said, "This is what you call focking money? Eh?" and hit me once again on my head with the firearm. The other man was trying to tie my hands behind my back with the telephone cord he had ripped out of the wall in the office.

I was sitting there and the leader was talking to somebody on his cell phone, standing in front of me when I said, "Where is my wife?" He stopped his phone call and said, "Don't worry about your focking wife. We dun kill she already. She in the car to go. Don't worry about she, worry about you! Today you go' dead!" I cannot begin to explain how I felt when he said they had killed Jennifer. At that moment, I felt I really had nothing to lose anymore.

I then said, "Well, well, well, look where I reach. Do you know who I am? All my life, for the past 50 years, I have worked defending people for serious crime like murder and so, and you come here to do this to my wife and myself? Well, well, well. I really reach!" One of them said, "Well boy, tomorrow somebody will have to represent somebody else for murdering you, because you will dead today!"

It was just about 6:00 am, and I was resigned to the belief that I was going to be murdered. I closed my eyes and asked Almighty God for forgiveness and awaited the gunshot. When the leader said, "Come go!" I braced for the shot, but it did not come.

About ten seconds later, I opened my eyes and realized they were gone. I immediately opened the office window and shouted to the neighbors, *"Help! Help! Help!"* In a few minutes, they were in our home. Jennifer came out of the toilet where she was hiding, and I cannot begin to tell you how I felt when I saw her. She was very badly beaten up, but she was alive. Thank God!

Jennifer was beaten up so badly that it took a few months for her to recover. The Leader had kicked her in the stomach area and her entire stomach was swollen and black and blue for weeks.

After about four months, Jennifer's stomach began swelling and we were advised to go to the USA for treatment. When we arrived there, tests were done and we were informed that she had cancer of the peritoneum, a very rare form of cancer. She died on the 24th of January 2016. A mere nine months after she was beaten up.

After Jen died, I asked the surgeon in charge of her case whether he thought the beating was the cause of her death. His reply to me was, "Mr. De Lima. I am confident that the beating was what brought it about. The gene was there but would most probably have remained dormant for years, had the beating not taken place."

Jennifer was cremated and I returned her ashes to Trinidad where she lies next to her dear mother Marjorie, in Mucurapo Cemetery.

Three months after the incident, I saw one of the two men who brutalized us. I was standing in the line to pay in Hi Lo, St. Augustine. He was the person ahead of me, We looked at each other and then he just left the line and quickly walked away.

As I write this, the women of Trinidad and Tobago are under siege. More than fifty of them, known to the police, are simply missing. They are afraid to go anywhere, anytime, by themselves, for fear that they will be attacked. It is almost as though they are considered second-class citizens. Shades of Afghanistan.

And the woman's age doesn't matter in the least. A seventy-year-old woman would be beaten up and ravished in the same way as a young girl of say sixteen would be. I experienced that with my dear wife Jennifer when they dealt with us.

I'm sure if the young women and girls of the U.K. were being slaughtered at the rate they are in Trinidad and Tobago nowadays, the English people would not only welcome, but they would demand, the return of the hangman. Yet we are bombarded every so often by the English to remember not to reimpose the Death Penalty in Trinidad and Tobago. I really don't think they like us.

There is little respect, if any at all, for our women folk. Year in and year out we witness them being raped, brutalized, and murdered, and very little is done about it. It is sickening to think like that but it is the truth. Many such cases are relegated to the inner pages of our dailies and very often the word 'Murder' is replaced by the word 'Killing', which is meant to make it more acceptable to the reader. To soften the blow, as it were.

So very many Ladies have had their lives brutally 'snuffed out' in recent days. I cry for all of them, including the Japanese artist and guests to Trinidad, ASAMI, ANDREA BHARATH, REHANA JAGGERNAUTH, KEZIA JENELA GUERRA, ABIGAIL LEWIS, and INDRA JAGROOP. But most of all, I cry for Trinidad and Tobago.

I live in the USA now because all my children and grands live there, and I am coming to the end of my life. I have loved Trinidad all my life and I always shall.

But I cry for Trinidad all the time. The people of Trinidad are, by and large, the kindest, most loving and considerate in the whole world. That is what is so hard. To see these people just having to take and take and take whatever the criminals dish out, is so sickening.

From a little boy, I was taught by my father that "Right is Right, and Wrong is Wrong." I have tried to live by that motto.

All those lovely people who continue to strive to make Trinidad and Tobago a better place for our children, I salute you. Phillip Alexander, Fr. Hugh Joyeaux, Wayne Chance, Richard Barker, Pastor Clive Dottin, Hoolsie Bhaggan, Rhonda Maingot and Sharon Inglefield are but a few of those.

God Bless all of you. But I tell you honestly, evil is amongst us – from the highest to the lowest. People are afraid to complain because corruption has ascended to the ruling ranks. It is widely believed that wealth and position absolves all wrongdoing. Our judicial system is in trouble and there is a *bete gote* attitude that prevails.

Criminals sit at table with some of the high society of the country and some of the politicians are themselves criminal – unable to travel outside of Trinidad and Tobago for fear of being arrested. And one shudders to think that the children growing up today will be asked to emulate those types. Why doesn't our Government give up those folks, voluntarily? I tried my best to be of assistance when I lived there. I even offered myself for the politics of the country. But from very early on, it was pellucidly clear that people go into politics in Trinidad and Tobago to steal. And it is almost as though it is expected. So for anyone who has any modicum of integrity, that is certainly no place to find yourself.

I have lived a very exciting life. I have been blessed by being so fortunate to have had such a good wife and companion as Jennifer, who has given me four good children and seven wonderful grandchildren.

A good friend asked me recently, "Vernon, what have you taken away from having practiced law for fifty years?" I thought carefully about the question, and the answer is...I learnt a number of lessons, but the two that jump out immediately are (1) *Never judge a book by its cover*, and (2) *Right is right and wrong will always be wrong.*

My Senior in Chambers, Mr. Bruce McIntosh Procope, was a very wise man who grew up on the folklore of Trinidad and Tobago. Some of his expressions were as absolutely priceless as they were instructive:

- "Nought is never in danger."
- "When in doubt, the answer is NO!"
- "Play to the pitch of the ball."
- "Take a fresh guard."
- "New ball soon lose its shine."

Those are a few of his sayings. How fortunate I was to be accepted into his Chambers. I learnt so very much from him. Growing up I was lucky to meet and befriend many good and sincere people who remained my friends for life.

The island of Antigua holds a special place in my heart for two very good reasons. The first and more important is that four of my best friends and their wives, Derek and June Marcano, Ferdi and Angie De Gannes, David and Dawn Camacho and Hugo and Maria Ross all resided there, and secondly, the beaches, all 365 of them, are the most beautiful in the world.

Jennifer and I visited them on two occasions, and we had an absolute ball each time.

CHAPTER 34

WHY I WALKED AWAY

I did so because I felt there was nothing more I could do to help with the situation in Trinidad. I tried with all my force to no avail.

Over the years, I witnessed so many great Trinidadians toil and toil for our country, only to end up broken and laughed at, and in some cases ridiculed and scorned, for doing and/or speaking what was manifestly the right thing.

Gene Miles comes to mind right away. She was a bright and beautiful woman who died in the gutters of Port of Spain for telling the truth. Albert 'Bertie' Gomes, one of the most important political personalities of our country was hounded out of Trinidad when the PNM won its first Election in 1957. He and his entire family were exiled to England to spend the final years of his life. This man who had devoted most of his life for the betterment of Trinidad and Tobago, and greatly assisted in the advancement of the Steel Band and Calypso, lived and died like a pauper in England, a country he fought tooth and nail against, over the many years, on behalf of the people of Trinidad and Tobago.

And my dear and honorable friend, Dr. Morgan Jobe, whom I called to his face: **The John the Baptist of Trinidad and Tobago Politics.** What a wonderful man. He worked so hard trying to educate the people of our country, but they poured scorn on him. I was privileged to have known him and I am certain that one day soon, his teachings will be commonplace in the education curricula of Trinidad and Tobago.

All those persons, and there are so many more, lived for Trinidad and Tobago, but they died heartbroken because their words fell on deaf ears. And I witnessed this with many others who suffered the same fate. With God's leave, I'll see them in Heaven.

I pray for Trinidad every day. I pray that all will be well soon again with the country, and that Almighty God, whom I do not believe is a Trinidadian, will protect us against Hurricanes and Earthquakes and all that is evil, including corrupt politicians, professionals and other bad individuals.

Finally, to the little boy who pointed to me and said, "Mummy, look Dole Chadee lawyer," I say this, "True, I was Dole Chadee's lawyer, but more important, I was a lawyer. I represented anybody who needed my help, whether they were guilty or not guilty. I did my job forcefully and conscientiously, and I enjoyed every moment of doing it." As I said before, I was amazed that people were willing to pay me for what I would have done for free.

I believe I have spoken enough. This was my *Closing Address*. I now rest my case!

My dear friend Dr. Morgan Jobe

EPILOGUE

This is my Closing Address because I shall never address the people of Trinidad and Tobago again. This then is my parting salvo, intended to share with you some of my experiences over the past sixty years, which I believe have been vital years in the development of Trinidad and Tobago. I am in the Departure Lounge at this time.

What caused our country to turn into a dangerous place is really Everybody's business. It did exactly that. To a great extent we, its citizens, are responsible because we saw it coming from a long way off and we did absolutely nothing to stop it. I give it as I got it, nothing more, nothing less.

In the course of my lifetime, so many important events have occurred that no doubt added fuel to the fire of the Nation's downfall.

To name a few:

— Gene Miles and the Gas Station Racket
— The Lock Joint Scandal
— The D.C. 9 Affair

- The 1970 Mutiny of the Soldiers
- The attempted overthrow of the Government by Abu Bakr and his thugs
- The Prevatt and Ou Wai Scandal
- La Tinta
- The C.L Financial Fiasco
- Calder Hart
- Temple in the Bush
- The Petrotrin Affair

These, which were all mishandled if ever handled at all, are but a few I now recall, but what is clear is that the people we entrusted to take care of us over the years have not only ignored us, but in fact have been the ones who pillaged the innocent and trusting people of Trinidad and Tobago. There never ever seemed to be any sincere resolution on the part of the authorities to deal with such matters at all. It got to the stage where we all accepted the adage – "Well this is Trinidad, and of course, we are nine-day wonder people, not so?" "Ent?" And one of our Government Ministers went so far as to say: "All of we tief!" I can assure the reader that that is not so!

Our politicians, on both sides, have in fact betrayed the people big time. To the extent that they have collectively brought us to the brink of national disaster. And do you think they care? Not one damn bit. As a result, over the years we, the voter folk, have come to understand the despise that the politicians have for us, and so we have lost all respect for them. That is the reason very, very few decent people care to offer themselves for political office in Trinidad and Tobago.

I love Trinidad and Tobago, and I feel so sad that I cannot return home at this time. But maybe some day things will be different. Whatever should happen, let me be very clear, that to my mind there is no better place on earth than our two Islands. But our people must stand up and fight to restore their majesty. "You have eyes to see" (a great saying), so don't let down the side!

If I may have written in this book about any matter that may be considered offensive to anyone, I say to you I am sorry for that was not my intention. I merely wished to relate as best as I could some of my interesting experiences when I practiced in Trinidad and Tobago.

Finally, I wish to say that whatever monies that may be derived from the sales of this book I shall direct to be paid to a designated trustee for, and on behalf of, the so many vagrants of our cities. In other words, this book and all its proceeds belong to the Vagrants of Trinidad and Tobago.

And at all times I keep in mind the old adage:

"There, but for the grace of God, go I."

[Illustration on following page of my Jennifer]

My lovely Jennifer, as I will always remember her